Praise

'There has never been a better time to be an entrepreneur as AI levels the playing field for SMEs to compete. Chris Davies is a visionary pioneer and smart technologist who understands this space more than anyone else I know. When Chris talks business, technology and all things innovation – I listen!'
  — **Alan Smith**, CEO, Capital Asset Management

'The financial services world is just at the beginning of realising the huge potential of combining behavioural science, data analytics, machine learning and technology to improve human decision-making. Chris has brought together these themes into practical strategies for companies to turn these buzzwords more effectively into business success.'
  — **Dr Greg B Davies**, Head of Behavioural Finance, Oxford Risk

'Model Office regtech has helped us maintain a compliant, sustainable and multi-award-winning business. This book provides an intuitive strategy and framework for any business (big or small) who wants to ensure they are on the right track in embedding technology and AI into their systems and controls and services.'
  — **Andrew Elson**, CEO, Berry & Oak Chartered Financial Planners

'To build a culture that embraces data and AI, organisations must invest in and learn how to use these technologies effectively. A great way to start is with this must-read book, as Chris Davies gives clear examples and case studies of proven strategies for any business leader seeking to understand and adopt the potential for building groundbreaking businesses, disrupting old-school models and embracing the benefits of real-time, highly accurate data for the good of both company and client.'

— **Lee Robertson**, CEO, Octo Members

Chris Davies

Culture Coding

Harness technology, artificial intelligence and behavioural science to empower your business culture and performance

R^ethink

First published in Great Britain in 2023
by Rethink Press (www.rethinkpress.com)

This book is dedicated to Maev Creaven, who was a shining light and advocate for evidence-based practice in the nutritional and functional medicine profession and one of the most beautiful souls I have ever had the privilege and honour to have met.

Contents

Foreword

C hris has for many years been well ahead of new and emerging trends and technologies, waiting patiently for the world to catch up.

Not so long ago, talk about artificial intelligence (AI) seemed the province of nerdy academia, with little real-world application or understanding. Now we are wondering if we should simply ask ChatGPT what it would like us to do and when it wants to take over.

For those of us left who feel honour-bound to try and control and use technology rather than surrender and be trampled over by it, Chris offers a yoke to place around its neck. We may be unable to control all of the wild excesses of technology, but the great leaps forward in physics and biology didn't see us destroy the universe, so there is no reason the AI revolution can't be a force for good as well.

Phil Young, Managing Partner of Zero Support

Introduction

There is no getting away from the fact that technology is now a fundamental part of life. Whether you are driving your car using satnav, buying a book online (hopefully this one) or editing your smartphone photographs, you are using sophisticated yet relatively cheap technology.

Technology is not magic, but it might seem to be that way; the ability to do far more with less must have seemed miraculous to anyone born in the 1950s and 60s – the baby boomers. When they were teenagers, there was no internet and televisions were the break-through technology. Now we can develop our own technology platforms and run business meetings online, which helped us to not only survive but thrive through a pandemic that no one foresaw back in 2019.

This book is all about how start-ups, small and medium-sized enterprises (SMEs), and, indeed, some multinational enterprises (MNEs) can review strategies and 'war stories' about the pros and cons of applying technology and AI, and gain significant competitive advantage while building and maintaining a constructive client- and staff-centred culture. I draw heavily on my personal experiences with retail financial services and in the wealth management industry where I have worked for significant corporations and small businesses, combining financial advice, private wealth management and strategic consultancy to explore how the framework we used to build our regulation technology (regtech) business can help other businesses, no matter what industry they operate in, to ensure they do not miss out on the new technology-driven digital economy we now find ourselves in.

Culture coding is about applying technology and behavioural science within our five key tenets:

1. **Your focus** – strategic planning

2. **Your engagement** – stakeholders such as clients, regulators and board members

3. **Your people** – employees, recruitment, and training and development

4. **Your systems** – operations, controls and data

5. **Your promise** – your service and product proposition

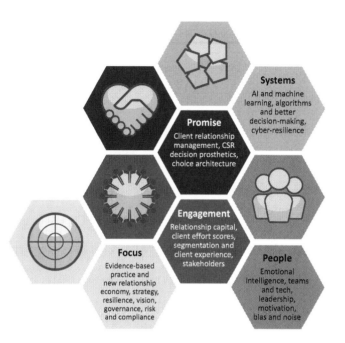

These five keys can empower sustainable performance while driving efficiencies of scale across organisations, without sacrificing hard-won client trust and business ethics. I will discuss each key in full in the second half of the book.

How to use this book

Given that we now live in a world of sound bites and instant information, I have structured the book into two parts with key themes. Part One, 'The Tenets Of Technology, AI And Behavioural Science', covers the case for engaging the digital revolution and behavioural science strategies. Part Two, 'The Five Culture

Code Keys', covers each of the principal strategies businesses need to engage to build a constructive culture and become a digital-led organisation.

Feel free to dip in and out of areas of interest depending on your business and/or personal preferences. For example, if you are an established business, you may not need to read the book from start to finish, preferring to focus on the areas that are most relevant to your interests or any challenges you currently face. If you are running a new business, you may want to dive straight into the five culture code keys. It is up to you; my only wish is that you gain at least one valuable insight that will make a positive difference to your business. If that is the case, then writing the book has been worth my while.

PART ONE

THE TENETS OF TECHNOLOGY, AI AND BEHAVIOURAL SCIENCE

ONE

What Is Technology And Why Should You Engage?

Two questions for you: for how long did humans use horses as their main mode of travel, and how long did it take for the car to take over once invented? The answers may surprise you. The adoption of the horse as the main form of transport can be traced back to (at least) 3,000 BCE when, according to archaeologists, horse domestication may have begun in Kazakhstan.[1] Developments such as wagons in the American West and carriages in Europe revolutionised mass travel. This led, in turn, to the development of the first automobiles and the German engineer Carl Benz applying for a patent for his 'vehicle powered by a gas engine' in 1886. By 1908 entrepreneurs like Henry Ford were mass producing cars, which quickly began to take off thanks to cities being designed around car transport. This meant that in New York City it took just fifteen years for the car to completely replace the horse as the main means of travel.

Five thousand years of horse-enabled travel being replaced by the motor car in less than two decades is impressive, but we can see similar examples of fast-moving innovation in business, with the development from paper mail to fax to email to social enterprise software, and human-powered jobs such as personal assistants, administrators and cashiers being replaced by technology empowered by AI. I could go on, but you get the gist: this book is all about how technology can act as a significant enabler to create the right culture across all your business services, products and operations, so you can gain more efficient results fast and move ahead of your competition in a positive, compliant and effective manner. As we are now in the 'fourth industrial revolution' (4IR) – that of the internet, digitisation and technology – your business model needs to be aligned to the latest advancements in technology if it is to thrive in the modern-day commercial environment. Let me put it this way: with 80% of jobs likely to be affected by AI, can you afford not to engage with 4IR?[2]

The concern over progressive technological innovation, and AI in particular, is that machine learning will replace human labour. There are now many technology professionals who want to put a stop, or at least a pause, to the use of advanced AI tools. This book encourages those working in industry to focus on how technology and AI can augment not supplant humans by enabling greater efficiencies, promoting productivity for the greater good, and allowing humans to focus more on the areas technology cannot easily replicate, such as soft skills and emotional intelligence.

We also need to consider the realm of practicality and whether AI-enabled work may reach saturation point. If we look at any technological progression within industry, such as self-service checkout points, apps to enable instant purchase, or automated telecommunication software – all designed to reduce time and costs and increase demand – the direct impact of these types of customer service innovation is what is called the 'inverted-U curve': as technology progresses, it can stimulate employment but then drive it down.[3] It follows that the relationship between technology advances and employment rates depends on where we are on the inverted-U curve; for example, if technology increases performance but significantly eases pressure on performance, this can drive down productivity overall. In other words, there is a performance threshold point, after which humans can become lazy.

The key to understanding technology and how it could help your business is to recognise that your current business methodology and culture require continuous measured change to ensure you stay competitive and relevant to your clients. We've witnessed countless glaring examples of organisations ignoring technology advancements (and business sense in some cases) at their peril. Think of a leading telecommunications business, whose phones had a 50%

share of the market in 2007 but who failed to adapt to the new smartphone lifestyle product; or the owners of high street stores who, rather than develop their own e-commerce model, signed a deal with a leading online shopping platform who were already using other, similar vendors.

Technology as an enabler

Let us remain positive: technology, implemented carefully and correctly, can save businesses significant costs and time, leading to transformational results. Built well, it is an 'enabler' tool which can allow us to work more effectively and efficiently, and gain quality data and management information (MI) so we can track trends across key metrics. It is helpful to review certain aspects of technology that firms should consider when creating a collaborative, client-centred culture that can support sustained success:

- **Cloud computing:** The cloud is simply a safe repository for data created by a global network of servers, each with a unique function. By transferring web-based data to the cloud for a monthly fee, your business can save on staff and maintenance, and benefit from frequent updates.

- **Open-source software (OSS):** A big problem with technology can be what is classed as 'legacy' technology, in which older and closed coding has been used, creating a 'black box' that is fettered and rigid, and difficult, sometimes impossible, to integrate with. If you are looking to the future and want to build your own proprietary technology or integrate with third parties, your technology has to offer OSS. This means software that is distributed with its source code so it is available for use, modification and distribution with its original rights. Developers can access OSS and adapt it to best fit the business's ongoing needs.

- **Software as a service (SaaS):** There are three services that a firm linked to cloud computing can employ. The most common is SaaS, which offers cloud-based tools and applications for everyday use. SaaS products are popular with businesses that want to grow and build. SaaS is highly scalable and easy to use and manage with instant upgrades. You will need to ensure due diligence is conducted to guarantee compatibility with existing technology. There is also platform as a service (PaaS), which provides a cloud-based platform mainly for developers to collaborate and build custom applications for dealing with storage, data serving and management. PaaS is brilliant if you want to build and host a technology platform for your staff or clients. Finally, infrastructure as a service (IaaS) helps you build, manage and control your data infrastructure, and physically manage it onsite. You then use APIs (explained below) to access and manage your resources.

- **Application programming interface (API):**
  This software-to-software interface provides a
  secure and standardised way for applications to
  work with each other, so collaboration is the key
  here. APIs essentially work via requests through
  third-party applications, such as uniform
  resource locators (URLs), dictated by the rules of
  hypertext transfer protocol (HTTP). Put simply,
  an API is a broker, a middle entity between the
  business and third-party software and its server,
  completing information requests and providing
  them to the business in a meaningful format, and
  creating valuable MI and data for the business to
  offer to third parties.

- **AI:** Do not be afraid. We cover AI in depth later,
  but automation is the way forward when it
  comes to streamlining your business services
  and products. I suspect you already employ AI;
  just think about organising your email, apps to
  help manage cash flow and invoicing, and satnav
  tools. I could go on. Carefully deployed, AI and
  the latest machine learning large language model
  (LLM) platforms can help your business become
  more efficient in its key activities, such as report
  writing, compliance audits and chatbot-driven
  client signposting. They also eliminate human
  error, thus optimising key business processes and
  reducing overheads while keeping you ahead
  of the competition and increasing quality data
  and MI.

- **Client relationship management (CRM) software:** These platforms have revolutionised client service and analytics. Used correctly, this technology will deepen client relationships, provide data evidence and MI, and cut marketing and administration costs.

- **Video conferencing software:** Think how you survived the recent lockdowns and stayed on your feet as a business. Teleconferencing and webinars have empowered home working and 'hybrid' working, thus making it easy to ensure staff and clients are supported and costs and time are saved by reducing travel.

- **Blockchain:** A distribution ledger technology (DLT) is essentially a platform that allows independent computers (nodes) to record, share and synchronise transactions such as financial investments. Blockchain is a DLT subset that allows transactions to be stored in the form of chains of blocks, and each block produces a unique hash that can be used as proof of valid transactions. Each node has a copy of the ledger, which helps to make it transparent. The advantages of using blockchain are numerous, but principally it decentralises the DLT and provides complete transparency and ease of transfer across different technology platforms in a safe manner.

There are many more examples, and it is worth conducting a cost benefit analysis for the technology that you currently employ. The results will show you how efficient you have become and allow you to compare what you are using with other similar technology to see whether change is required.

Technology is not magic

It is also important to realise what technology is not, and it is certainly not magic. This is where software businesses who sell themselves as a 'silver bullet' suffer. Technology should not be viewed as a panacea, something that just appears and at the click of a button provides all the solutions we need to make business services and products more effective and efficient.

Built well, technology requires hard work to ensure it is fit for purpose and can live up to the billing of supporting business behaviours and developing staff skills to create a client-centred culture.

I hear too often that technology is mis-sold and does not live up to its hype when applied within the business service or operations. It is important to mention that well-designed technology needs time to embed into the business so staff are confident and competent using it and clients can see the ongoing benefits – something we'll touch on shortly. This goes for existing or legacy systems, or technologies that you are looking to replace with new technology. You need to avoid key risks, such as lost data or information, service outages or, worse still, system blackouts that are detrimental or sometimes terminal to a business and its clients.

What technology essentially does for business is enable certain key functions to work quicker and better so products and services are delivered faster and more effectively, accurate communications, data and MI are collated and delivered correctly, and evidence-based practice (EBP) is embedded, as in our company mantra: 'If you do not have the data, it did not happen and if you do have it, it better have happened!'

At this stage, whether you are new to technology or not, it is worth spending a bit of time on research and a due diligence strategy across certain types of technology and software design to learn how you can ensure that any technology is the right fit for your organisation.

Generative AI in action

We now have plenty of hype and fads to contend with (think 3D printing), and some of the AI machine learning offerings are one example of these; however, the LLM 'AI for the masses' is impressive. Let me show you how: the paragraphs below were generated from my ChatGPT machine learning platform account query, 'What is generative AI?'

> *Generative AI is a subset of machine learning that involves using algorithms to generate new content, such as images, music, text, or even videos. Unlike traditional machine learning algorithms that are trained on large datasets and used to make predictions*

based on that data, generative AI models are trained to create entirely new content based on the patterns and structures present in the data.

Generative AI can be divided into two main categories: discriminative models and generative models. Discriminative models are used to classify or recognize data, while generative models are used to create new data. Some common examples of generative AI include:

Image synthesis: Generative models can be trained to create realistic images that look like they were taken by a human photographer. These models can be used for a variety of applications, from generating realistic training data for computer vision algorithms to creating virtual worlds for video games.

Text generation: Generative models can also be used to create new text, such as news articles, product descriptions, or even entire novels. These models are often used in natural language processing applications, such as chat bots or virtual assistants.

Music composition: Generative models can be used to compose new pieces of music, either by mimicking the style of a particular composer or by creating entirely new compositions based on patterns and structures found in existing music.

Video generation: Generative models can also be used to create new videos, either by combining existing video clips or by creating entirely new video content based on patterns and structures found in existing videos.

The message here is that although AI can deliver some impressive results, it still needs to be trained. We incorporate generative AI into our compliance chatbot, and it takes effort to ensure it does not go 'off-piste' and 'hallucinate' with the considerable knowledge bank it has to call on. Machine learning suffers from hallucinations such as making up information (think fake news) and getting facts wrong. It's not perfect and needs training to deliver accurate information. It is also not (yet) sentient, but, used within systems and controls, AI can provide significant benefits to your business if you apply a robust research and due diligence strategy.

Research and due diligence

A good place to start is with your business plan (hopefully you have one). This is a road map through your business goals (short term) and objectives (medium to long term), your products and services, governance and risk management, employees and client engagement. It is all about knowing where you are and where you need to be, and tracking the technologies that you currently do or do not have that can enable your desired outcomes.

A technology road map is essential. This can be applied across the five keys we discuss in this book to keep you and your team on track, ensuring you have the right technology and approaches to achieve your aspirations. A road map should incorporate the main deliverables, systems and processes over the medium to long term, and the participants responsible for the design, delivery and implementation stages.

A road map can provide all stakeholders with an in-depth understanding of:

- A timeline of steps and phases to implementation along with resources required

- All existing and legacy technology with key features and cost benefit analysis

- New technology solutions with key features and cost benefit analysis, software migration

- Whether the existing technology stack (tech stack) is fit for purpose and, if not, which improvements are required

- Operational resilience and business continuity that the technology provides, scenario testing, critical challenges in the event of disruptions, relationships with the tech stack

- Important business services that are influenced by technology

- Costs associated with maintenance and IT upgrades

- How to unify disparate systems

- The development work required for technology to meet ongoing requirements

Prior to implementing any technology, a firm should always gain a granular understanding of its own IT systems and architecture. The due diligence process should start with existing software and hardware systems, by assessing their effectiveness, sustainability and ability to integrate with other services. It should cover:

- Hardware and software systems, ideally starting with OSS

- Technology flow and architectural charts

- Cloud platforms

- Web servers

- Product designs

- APIs

There needs to be a clear rationale for how existing or new technology empowers current and future business products, services, operations and maintenance requirements, and for how efficiencies are gained – for example, across costs and time.

Next, we have intellectual property (IP). Proprietary software will add significant value to your company, so if you are going down the route of developing your own technology, then key areas such as patents, copyright and trademarks should all be correctly applied for and protected, and you should ensure that third-party rights (for example, those of your competitors or clients) are not infringed, causing ownership and legal issues.

If applying third-party technology, then part of the contractual agreement should acknowledge who owns the IP and how this is dealt with over time.

Outsourcing

It also makes sense for businesses to outsource to third-party technology providers where they do not have a solution or the skills or funds to build one. Cloud computing is the best example: moving away from the costs and risks of hosting IT onsite to outsourcing to a cloud server solution. The key here is to carefully manage all relational and business risks by employing a stepped strategy to continually assess outsourcing agreements and performance.

The due diligence steps a firm should take to ensure outsourced relationships are monitored and managed are crucial to risk management. Each of the following components needs careful consideration when researching, onboarding and managing outsourced technology tools:

- **Role ownership:** A gatekeeper is chosen for the outsourced relationship(s) across roles and responsibilities and is accountable and responsible for ongoing risk management.

- **Contract:** This should be clear and understood by all stakeholders and reviewed at least annually. It should define where services are communicated clearly, including exit terms, continuity and contingency arrangements.

- **Service level agreement:** As with the contract, this needs to be clear, understood and reviewed. It should set out service time frames, reporting and escalation requirements.

- **Key performance indicators (KPIs) and key risk indicators (KRIs):** Both are agreed, and accountability across action planning for performance and risk-management metrics, such as data security for firms outsourcing to the 'cloud' and other third-party IT services, is of paramount importance.

- **Service review meets:** These align the contract obligations with clear responsibility for relationship management and accountabilities across KPIs / KRIs. Along with regular reviews, they should provide time frames, agendas, documented evidence and governance reviews.

- **Periodic reviews:** These should take an evidence-based approach, with the minutes of all meetings recorded centrally and aligned with the contract and operational resilience annual review rule.

One of the key issues with outsourcing your technology to third parties is operational resilience, which means having a strategy in place to handle challenges such as blackouts (total loss) or brownouts (controlled and partial loss).

With a technology research and due diligence strategy, a road map and outsourcing risks considered, you will then have a choice: do it yourself or use third-party technology? This all depends on your business plan and objectives. Obviously, building your own proprietary technology can be the most rewarding given you should own the IP, yet joint ventures and partnerships can also provide huge benefits in pushing the business forward quickly; for example, by diversifying distribution internationally so it gains more capital and cash flow to build out other services and products to serve its clients.

Technology and culture coding

Technology can bind the five culture code keys together to produce an 'operating system' that powers the organisation. If technology is implemented carefully and used wisely, and a tech stack integrates seamlessly, then this can improve staff retention. Social enterprise technology can promote learning and empower employees' career development, and CRM can offer clients clear information and 'turnkey' solutions that enable them to engage with ease. Regtech can enable quality MI and data for boards and executives to make informed choices and follow EBP, ensuring this culture coded operating system is functional and working to support the business goals while keeping it compliant and profitable.

When we deal with bias and noise later, we will see that technology has a big part to play in identifying dysfunctional behaviours and dealing with them early, ensuring boards are diverse and communications cascade from top to bottom and vice versa so the business can work constructively and rationally to support clients and meet business goals.

What I call the new relationship economy (NRE) means that in an age of personalisation, clients want to have products and services tailored to their ongoing needs and are attracted to organisations that can prove they have their best interests at heart. In a survey by Jobvite, 46% of job seekers cite company culture as very important when choosing to apply to a company.[4] Those firms who can build a client-centred culture do so with technology at the centre of their business, streamlining services and products, communications and support so clients are confident that the business is there for them and built around their needs.

It is also true that happy and healthy employees generally mean a happy and healthy business.

Chapter checkpoints

- Carefully plan and map technology prior to implementation.

- Embrace the benefits of AI and take advantage of the administrative and more menial tasks it can perform to allow you to focus on the more emotional engagement aspects, such as client or staff engagement.

- Always ensure you have a research and due diligence strategy incorporating the points made in this chapter, road map the technology journey and get your team on board.

- If outsourcing, cover all research and due diligence points.

- Embrace technology across the five culture code keys and view them as an operating system that binds the business together.

TWO
What Is Corporate Culture?

Students of organisational development describe culture in many ways. It is often seen as the glue that holds organisations together,[5] which presents a real issue when we are faced with change and a new regulatory environment.

If we apply social science, much of the cultural background is tacit and concerned with the beliefs, habits and attitudes of the workforce. It can operate almost as the organisation's subconscious. The fact that culture is taken for granted means that behavioural science can help to facilitate an understanding of cultural drivers and also play a role in cultural change. In his work, Schein describes culture as 'deeper levels of basic assumptions and beliefs... that operate unconsciously'.[6] He distinguishes three levels of culture:

1. **Basic underlying assumptions** – beliefs, unconscious thoughts and feelings that are not visible or accessible, but taken for granted

2. **Organisational values** – the explicit strategies, goals and philosophies that organisations use to justify actions

3. **Artefacts** – visible organisational structures and processes

The social scientist Geert Hofstede conducted one of the most comprehensive studies into how values in the workplace are influenced by culture.[7] Where organisational culture is concerned, it is the practices that these organisations exhibit that matter.

Hofstede and Bob Waisfisz developed the organisational cultural model with six autonomous dimensions and two semi-autonomous dimensions, which outline the dynamics for cultural development based on principles of practice. In essence, this describes the way in which members of the organisation relate: to each other, their work and the outside world. This then distinguishes them from other organisations.

HOFSTEDE AND WAISFISZ'S SIX AUTONOMOUS AND TWO SEMI-AUTONOMOUS DIMENSIONS[8]

Autonomous dimensions

1. Means-orientated versus goal-orientated:
   The means is the 'how', and generally risk-avoidant; the goal is the 'what' and involves risks.

---

2. Internally versus externally driven: In an internally driven culture, employees perceive their tasks as givens; an external culture is completely driven by the customer.

3. Easy-going versus strict: In an easy-going culture the structure, control and discipline are loose, compared to the opposite in a strict environment.

4. Local versus professional: Local cultures give rise to a homogeneous workforce; professional cultures promote individuality and initiative.

5. Open versus closed system: This establishes the level of accessibility of the organisation to both insiders and outsiders.

6. Employee- versus work-orientated: In an employee-orientated workplace, management focus is on a personal, tailored, staff-centred approach, compared to a work-orientated culture that puts pressure on staff to perform tasks.

Semi-autonomous dimensions

1. Leadership style acceptance: This looks at the staff's preference for and acceptance of the leadership style in their workplace.

2. Identification with organisation: It is important to understand the degree to which staff identify with the organisation in its totality.

Driving constructive culture

If we accept the meaning of culture as a 'corporate glue', then we can begin to define strategies that help create a positive or constructive culture and encourage decision-making; we can create a 'reflexive' or sense-making culture based on recognition of biases at play, and steering strategies such as mission statements, nudges, technology and corporate philosophy, which build a positive and constructive values programme. The table below highlights examples of how identifying 'programmed biases' and using steering strategies can gain better cultural outcomes.

Technology and culture

Technology can take a cross-sectional review of business operations, people, financials and customers to gain a holistic view of the current organisational culture. This provides reliable information on the culture that should be driving staff behaviours (ideal culture), the culture that is driving biases and behaviours (current culture), the causal factors and levers for change that create and reinforce or modify the current culture, and the outcomes that result from that culture. This is, in essence, good corporate governance in action. Using this information, leaders can assess whether the current culture is a liability or an asset, and identify areas for change and ways to align

Driving constructive culture

Steering strategy	Programmed behavioural biases	Actions	Cultural outcome
Moral coding and accountability	Herding, heuristics, bad habits	Focus groups on coding strategy for corporate strategic planning	Stakeholder adherence to mission, values and philosophy, reduction in taking shortcuts
Nurturing and reward	Risk aversion, cognitive dissonance	Targeted praise, recognition and measured support through failures and successes	Happy workforce: self-confidence in abilities, career paths and skills, team ethics and affiliation
Endowment effect	Loss aversion, sunk cost	Encourage innovation, ownership and skills for tasks	Ownership and pride for role and tasks in hand
Focusing	Status quo, inertia, herding	Tight attention to tasks in hand, timelines and small wins	Efficient, streamlined engagement, low bottlenecks and stagnation, time-bound and creating winning mentality
Blue-sky thinking and widening the repertoire	Narrow framing, 'halo' effect	Broad framing of key strategies, operations and tasks against the environment and market	Holistic engagement of internal and external issues, releases, internal and external resources, and team potential, plus avoids 'groupthink'
True transparency	Saliency, cognitive dissonance	Clear communication channels, constructive challenge, clarity of message and tasks	Consistent, accountable, dependable decisions and 'walking the talk'

the organisation's mission, goals, objectives and philosophies with day-to-day activities. They can also quantify the impact for practical change initiatives and interventions.

There are six areas a business should consider:

1. Identify the ideal culture – in my company we class constructive culture as client-centric, affiliative, focused on staff needs, aspirational and achievement-orientated.

2. Identify the risks to this ideal culture – roles, responsibilities, poor communications.

3. Empower individual accountability – training and development.

4. Employ mechanisms to improve risk management – risk technology.

5. Employ strategic oversight – functional and diverse board membership.

6. Assess activities that could undermine risk management – remuneration, compliant procedures, barriers to good client outcomes.

Technology has a role to play across all six areas. It can diagnose the ideal corporate culture, then perform a gap analysis across risk management, ensuring staff accountabilities and responsibilities are clear and positively framed along with cascading communications throughout the organisation so staff are on the same page. Governance and oversight will then be empowered with quality data and MI that reflects cultural growth and evidences actions taken to encourage positive competence (skills) and conduct (behaviours) across the business.

This all means that technology can enable a firm to identify where they are 'at', the gaps that need to be addressed and the actions required to achieve sustainable success. With the five culture coding keys in mind, we can see that technology provides an important measuring tool, applying metrics and analytics to the organisation's cultural performance across staff behaviours, motivations, competence, client and stakeholder engagement. Technology also provides EBP to stop dysfunctional culture undermining business strategy.

Measuring and managing culture

To understand and improve culture we need to measure it. An awareness of what constitutes good and constructive culture is not enough; we need to deep dive into the psychological depths of the organisation to understand the impacts and levers for change where this is appropriate.

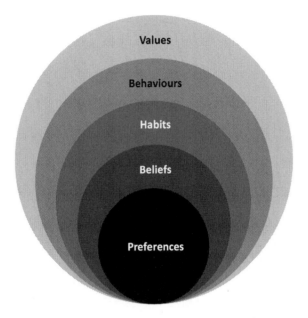

Levels of organisational cultural growth

Culture is difficult to measure due to models representing a simplification of reality and its subjective nature. We need to present an unbiased model and use diagnostics that provide good validity.

The figure above represents the classification for different levels of cultural growth. Given the importance of social science to our understanding of culture, we can see that the deeper we go, the more difficult it can be to change existing practices. The cultural variables are:

- **Values** – a sense of honour and duty

- **Behaviours** – actions based on beliefs and habits

- **Habits** – formed by shortcuts made in assessing information
- **Beliefs** – rules of thumb or freeze-dried reasoning can lead to incorrect beliefs
- **Preferences** – influenced by emotions and psychological experiences

Technology and diagnostic tools help with this. They must be well researched, grounded in EBP and supported by social science literature that is statistically validated, normed and proven by decades of use in the field. The relationship between the variables and effective culture has to be measured in a quantitative way. Using diagnostic tools can allow businesses to gain a better understanding of where the cultural gaps are and what to do about them.

Understanding behavioural bias

Back to the scientists. The behavioural-based experiments of social science greats such as Daniel Kahneman, Amos Traversky, Robert Thaler and Daniel Ariely have been well documented. They have found that our thinking is hijacked time after time by a 'behavioural imposter': the bias that can influence and skew our decision-making to cause irrational decisions and behaviour. One of my favourite experiments is commonly called 'endowment theory'[9] – or, as Ariely et al call it, the 'IKEA effect'[10] – whereby increased effort put into work tasks means increased attachment and associated recognition of such 'sweat equity', meaning we value something we own far more than something we do not. The way IKEA comes into this is if we buy and build something (eg a wardrobe) there is more ownership than if we didn't buy or build it. There is (sometimes literally) a piece of us in the process of building. It is the same with data, particularly if we apply gamification (more of this later). If we can assess our own data on a particular issue (eg culture) then we want to see improvements to match our expectations and attachment to good outcomes.

THE IKEA EFFECT

Based on endowment theory, research shows that labour enhances affection for its results; people overvalue their creations.

This can also mean loss aversion and sunk cost effect due to resources given to failing projects, and that third-party ideas are discounted over internally developed ones.

Other biases include cognitive dissonance. For example, knowing what we need to do to live a healthy life or run a successful business is relatively obvious; the test is making it happen. The key here is the tension that arises between beliefs and behaviour. We know that something may not be working for us in the long term, but we tend to continue to be seduced by its short-term gratification.

There are plenty of resources out there in the world of behavioural psychology that list our biases as they find them (and we will consider some of these in Chapter Eight). I do not find this as useful as it may appear, as humans can be a deceptive and unpredictable species, so psychology is not an exact science; but it's worth noting some key strategies that can help us examine, manage, monitor and improve organisational culture. As we can see from the figure below, preferences tend to be influenced by biases that are emotion-driven, thus giving a cause-and-effect relationship with beliefs, decisions and subsequent actions.

Preference	Beliefs	Decisions
Emotions and psychological experiences	Heuristics – rules of thumb, eg the way things are	Shortcuts, narrow framing, mental accounting

Biases and decision-making

Culture and bias

If we believe that culture represents 'the way we do things around here' and holds collective behaviour together, then we need to consider how culture affects bias and decision-making. Cultural bias, where psychology is concerned, is judging by standards inherent in your own culture. The management phrase 'groupthink' is an example of how this can manifest.

One of the most tragic examples is NASA and the ill-fated Space Shuttle Challenger mission, where engineers knew of faulty parts months before take-off but pushed ahead to avoid negative press. A culture that prioritised a good public relations strategy and meeting deadlines trumped risk and safety.

In any industry there are signs that a dysfunctional culture can cause serious risk. You only have to look at examples such as the financial crises of 2008–2009, which exposed corporate greed and businesses that exhibited:

- A domineering CEO or manager or group pressure

- Poor challenge to the board and committee and group decision-making favouring the status quo

- A lack of diversified or technical competence skill sets

If left unaddressed, such skewed biases and behaviour can only lead to poor performance, high risk and a destructive culture. Well-designed predictive algorithms can see patterns that humans cannot and provide solutions to resolve dysfunctional behaviours or poor decision-making. For example, medicine has seen progressive algorithms predicting signs of disease early, allowing doctors to diagnose and treat symptoms quicker and providing a better chance of patient survival. In another example, predictive analytics can combine data from multiple sources, such as medical records, fall detection pendants and medical alert services, which allows health providers to reach out to a senior person before a fall or medical complications. This in turn can prevent unnecessary hospital readmissions, reducing transport, acute care and rehabilitation costs.

This applies to any industry, including compliance activities in financial services, sports performance, and reducing the chance of pilot error in air travel.

Groups and bias

Along with groupthink, when people get together and interact within organisations, issues of herd, mob or pack mentality can arise, where people follow the leader and are influenced to adopt certain behaviours. This tends to be driven by base emotions such as greed and fear, and can be seen in situations such as mass investing creating bubbles and crashes. Where a firm's culture is concerned, it is important the right people are on board no matter how small the team is.

For sole traders or SMEs this could mean outsourcing certain services or products or hiring in expertise.

Bias and risk

Here's the rub: if we do not identify and get a grip on dysfunctional bias and its effect on decision-making processes, we create the high risk of a dysfunctional culture across the business and its development.

Remember the US secretary of State Donald Rumsfeld's quote? 'There are known knowns; there are things we know that we know. There are known unknowns… things that we know we don't know. But there are also unknown unknowns… things we don't know we don't know.'[11] This plays on the famous Johari window model developed by Joseph Luft and Harry Ingham in 1955 – a framework for understanding conscious and unconscious bias across the following areas:[12]

- Known to self and others = an open area, confirmed by experience

- Known to self, not known to others = an unseen area, so we can offer 'expertise'

- Not known to others, known to self = a hidden area, knowledge is often untapped

- Not known to others or self = unknown unknowns and hit hard by unseen challenges or threats

Politics aside, it is important that a business has the right risk-management culture installed, ideally from day one. If they do not, well, the risk is the business will fail fast and hard, not fail forward and learn.

Bias and noise

In his latest book, *Noise: A flaw in human judgment*, Daniel Kahneman and his collaborators, Olivier Sibony and Cass Sunstein, introduce the concept of background noise (inaccurate decision-making), which, along with the skewed thinking bias can bring, can affect and distort human decision-making.[13] We cover how technology can help alleviate such 'distractive' decision-making across this book, but it is important to mention that Kahneman and his colleagues see algorithms as one solution to supporting better decision-making and judgements. Obviously, we need to be aware that bias can also affect algorithm design, but, if factored in, predictive algorithms and the data they produce can provide us with themes and trends to ensure we know whether our business and its culture is on track.

Clients and bias

With client relationships in mind, we may deduce that by measuring our business and client irrationality and providing strategies to steer client-centric operations that are conducive to long-term relationships, we can gain positive outcomes for both our business and our clients. To do this, we need to understand the client behavioural (not just the attitudinal) journey. In Chapter Nine we will consider the value of integrating client service propositions with nudges and steers to identify and manage potentially damaging behavioural biases. By ensuring that clients' decisions are in their best interests, we have not only happy clients but also happy regulators. Measuring client behaviours means morphing biases into metrics. By quantifying qualitative data, businesses can associate subjective human behaviours with objective conclusions so that they can assign and segment services accordingly. This brings efficiency to the business and product suitability to meet client needs.

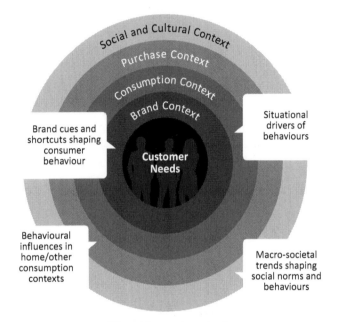

Social and Cultural Context

Purchase Context

Consumption Context

Brand Context

Brand cues and shortcuts shaping consumer behaviour

Customer Needs

Situational drivers of behaviours

Behavioural influences in home/other consumption contexts

Macro-societal trends shaping social norms and behaviours

Client bias and context

By focusing on context, marketeers and sales professionals can understand and structure product and service design to frame their offerings to appeal to and meet their customers' salient needs. Applying ethics and good corporate governance means these products and services will be transparent, will be understood and will offer value. It follows that client focus groups, surveys and carefully articulated client communications can help businesses with the key element: to understand and apply client context. A client-centred culture will certainly support this. In essence, business leaders need to become 'social scientists', and engage in controlled experiments to manage and monitor biases across their staff and clients.

Work and motivation

One of the key components for positive cultural growth is a happy workforce. In examining the drivers for this, we can embed the right practices, structures and incentives to provide a healthy work–life balance and meaning for the work in hand. Our work-based motivation equation provides an insight into the ingredients that need to be in play to stand a chance for good, healthy and happy work relationships.

> **WORK-BASED MOTIVATION EQUATION**
>
> Pride + reputation + purpose + meaning +
> camaraderie + fair remuneration
> = motivated workforce

The knock-on effect is obvious: a happy, motivated workforce means higher productivity, less illness, fewer days off sick and less negativity – all in all a happy and constructive culture. To get the mix right we have a number of factors to consider.

Monetary and social 'stress' and performance

This is where behavioural science plays a significant part in developing a constructive culture. The assumption has been that people are generically lazy and only work for money, yet this is only one motivator; people also enjoy the sense of purpose, winning and accomplishment that work gives them. This is dependent on a healthy balance between monetary and social recognition and reward. There are four points to note:

1. Roy Baumeister's work[14] looks at how willpower and ego depletion have a significant effect on developing culture. He finds that when we work hard our will capacity to perform at high standards drops as the hours go by.[15]

2. Albert Bandura's self-efficacy theory argues that our level of self-efficacy determines how we think, feel, motivate ourselves and behave.[16]

3. Fredrick Herzberg's motivation-hygiene theory reveals that certain characteristics of jobs consistently relate to job satisfaction.[17]

4. Abraham Maslow's work on motivation and needs suggests we strive to meet not only basic needs but also higher-order needs.[18]

It then follows that a well-incentivised, learned, positive and confident workforce full of self-belief will produce a constructive culture. How can this be achieved?

Work and money drivers

In his work, Daniel Ariely[19] has found that bonuses don't necessarily increase work satisfaction and wellbeing. When offered large financial rewards for performance, many people 'choked': performance got worse the higher the bonuses offered. This may mean that higher bonuses not only cost employers more but also that employers are not getting the most out of their executives.

Work and social drivers

Ariely's experiments extended to include social performance motivators such as public scrutiny, but again found that performance worsened in the public domain. The common denominator with money drivers was that, when skill became involved, this seemed to heighten anxiety and reduce performance accordingly.

Efficiency versus meaning

If money and public recognition aren't the performance panacea we think they are then what else can increase wellbeing? Helpful strategies include:

• Focusing on meaning so we have an opportunity to develop a real labour of love within corporate culture; the IKEA effect provides people with meaning

* Managing cognitive dissonance where tensions can exist between beliefs and behaviours; identifying the habitual tensions within organisations can help to engage the workforce

* Introducing social norms such as remuneration via client satisfaction and loyalty, or providing holistic benefits (onsite massage, counselling services) to increase morale and performance

The value of self-worth

What does this mean in the real world? Well, it's clear that those businesses that place their staff needs front and centre of the firm's welfare are the ones that seem to thrive. In 2015 Dan Price, the boss of Gravity Payments, a card payments company in Seattle, USA, introduced a US$70,000 minimum salary for all his 120 staff. At thirty-one, Price had 'made it' – a millionaire business owner with his company gaining around 2,000 customers, and an estimated worth of millions of dollars. What makes Price different is his view on inequality in the USA. He says, 'We're glorifying greed all the time as a society, in our culture. And, you know, the *Forbes* list is the worst example – "Bill Gates has passed Jeff Bezos as the richest man." Who cares!?'[20]

If we return to social science, a study by the Nobel Prize-winning economists Daniel Kahneman and Angus Deaton looked at how much money the average American needs to be happy. Their research concluded that people's emotional wellbeing plateaued when they made $75,000.[21] After crunching his numbers, Price arrived at the US$70,000 figure. This meant a third of his employees would have their salaries doubled immediately. Five years later, Gravity's performance has transformed: the headcount has doubled, the value of payments that the company processes has gone from US$3.8 billion to US$10.2 billion, and more than 10% of the workforce are homeowners (up from 1%). Price obviously got flak (being called a communist by the media), but this shows that equalising pay across all his staff (including himself) and providing them with just enough to be happy and motivated has stimulated a culture for growth and happiness in his business.

'Great,' I hear you say, or maybe 'So what?' Well, this example shows the importance of pulling people together for a common cause, in this case self-worth. Yes, there were challenges around higher-paid employees proclaiming the equalisation of salary as unfair, yet the cumulative effect of addressing a fundamental need for the majority of the workforce meant that business profits surged along with staff wellbeing.

The traditional transactional model for remunerating staff on production alone does not necessarily translate into a sustainable constructive culture. Money is only one part of the equation, and Gravity's example illustrates that it is those firms who take a holistic approach across staff social and financial needs that can make a real difference to the business performance and staff welfare.

Staff buy-in can be driven by social perks that mean something to the individual person; this could be extended leave, leisure activity bonuses such as sports events or cinema tickets or even dinner at a special restaurant. The trick is for businesses to find out the financial and social triggers that matter. This will take some time, but knowing staff needs inside and outside the workplace is key, and it is those bosses who truly take an interest in their staff who can win here.

A technology strategy for cultural growth

With Hofstede and Waisfisz's cultural model in mind, we can see that how members of organisations relate to the outside world matters immensely to cultural outcomes. Building high-quality stakeholder and client relationships is a central strategy for positive and constructive culture.

Technology such as psychometrics that enable recruiters to assess personality, aptitude and general and emotional intelligence, along with using soft skills in interviews, can create a holistic framework to blend diagnostic technology and people skills and better assess candidate suitability.

Integrating technology strategy with cultural growth

Business area	Technology strategy	Value
Selection, training and competency	Psychometric tools ensure recruits have the correct client-facing skills and ongoing job learning incorporates soft and hard skills	An empowering culture means newcomers fit in and are made welcome and that skills are appropriate for roles and responsibilities
Ethics: social versus market norms	Social enterprise platforms can provide a balance between developing relationships and financial capital via corporate responsibility and ensure mission statements are applied	Increased social responsibility gives accountability and transparency to culture and can encourage corporate values that align behaviour and culture
Partnership and joint ventures	API integrations can encourage data sharing and positive third-party relationships that create mutual business opportunities	Defining the right fit for third-party integrations means the data and MI can encourage compliant and client-centred relationships
Products and services	Designed around client needs and delivered effortlessly via tech and a segmented strategy to meet clients' behavioural needs	Client buyer motivations, price sensitivities and propensities are integrated into the culture

(Continued)

(Cont)

Business area	Technology strategy	Value
Regulation, government and legal	Regtech can bring a comprehensive understanding of the impact of ongoing regulatory directives and government and legal policy	Fiduciary care and MI for external governance will bring compliant conduct and culture plus regtech creates a third line of defence
Third-party technology	Due diligence should be applied on new technology so that it fits the business and provides operational efficiency and client-centricity	Job design appropriate for new technologies brings agility and flexibility to corporate culture

There are two key areas to consider.

Employee engagement

Research has shown that high employee engagement leads to high performance and positive culture. Diagnostically assessing the type of culture in the organisation can then help to examine areas for focus, including motivation, satisfaction, loyalty, co-operation and teamwork.

By acknowledging the pressures of modern-day living and offering staff non-monetary perks such as holidays or flexible working hours, and providing recognition for hard work and loyalty, organisations will benefit from an enthused workforce who will contribute significantly to its ongoing success.

Client-centricity

It is clear that there is now a case for firms to develop long-term business strategy that places the client at the centre of all they do. The financial services market is homogenous and conservative in its philosophy. Most mission and vision statements are similar, yet it is those firms who embrace and develop a culture for trusted client relationships that will thrive.

By moving away from a transactional approach and applying behavioural science strategies and technology that focuses on client behaviours, organisations will demonstrate long-term cultural sustainability. By understanding how clients feel about the organisation through assessing client motivations to buy, sensitivities to pricing, and propensities to buy more or less, organisations can understand how much clients value their services and how loyal they are. This is essential not only to building a constructive client-centric culture, but also to the value of the business. It is those businesses that can demonstrate highly trusting and loyal client relationships that will be attractive to potential purchasers and other clients who want similar services.

Harnessing technology to create a constructive culture

The issue is that to build and sustain a constructive culture within your business, you need to constantly measure, monitor and improve it where necessary. One of the best ways to do this is to employ technology such as diagnostics, algorithms and machine learning. Remember: technology built well is an enabler for business and cultural growth.

Technology can provide businesses with all the data and MI they need to know they are on track across the five key business growth areas, and to identify where any potential weaknesses are and design interventions accordingly. If applied well, technology will provide EBP so decisions can be made on real-time data points that show trends and behaviours that are on or off track and provide pointers for change.

There are a number of ways technology can aid and facilitate a constructive corporate culture.

Democratisation of information

In their personal lives, people have become accustomed to having access to any piece of information they want at a moment's notice. This hasn't always been the case in the workplace. In the past, data was usually kept in the hands of a select few, and extracting and using that data in a meaningful way was a long, painful process. Modern enterprise technologies and applications are pushing access to data and information to the front lines.

Performance enablement

Measuring an employee's impact is more efficient and ultimately more effective thanks to tools and technology that allow firms to regularly capture and aggregate real-time information. This is also true for measuring the business performance against regulations, government policies and market moves. Financial technology (fintech), regtech, social enterprise and CRM platforms are just some examples of how technology can provide valuable instant data for firms to continuously assess and improve their performance against the market environment they operate in.

Opportunity creation

Using CRMs and client engagement tools to assess their experience can open up new markets and opportunities based on client propensities and sensitivities to the features and costs of products and services. Similarly, e-learning and social enterprise technology can help identify future talent for the business.

Chapter checkpoints

- Gain a comprehensive understanding of the culture you need and use technology and tools to measure where you are and any gaps that need to be addressed.

- Understand or recognise bias and noise as it plays out within your business and work out how they can be best managed through interventions such as training or algorithms to support rational decision-making.

- Work out what financial and social needs motivate your workforce, and get the balance right between transactional and social benefits. You never know, a staff member may prize family time more than a bonus payment.

- Align your technology with your business goals and desired culture.

- Use social science tools, such as controlled experiments, surveys and focus groups, to gain quality MI and incorporate it in building a constructive culture.

THREE

Fine-tuning Your Organisation

The glaring problem I see when presented with those who argue (some with red faces) that technology and AI will eradicate jobs and cause mass unemployment is that they are missing the fact that humans should focus on becoming more human. What I mean is, AI currently finds it incredibly difficult to detect emotions (despite some claims to the contrary). Think about the service industries: in healthcare, doctors, nurses and carers need to employ excellent bedside manners, and the financial services industry requires professional interpersonal soft skills such as active listening and open questioning.

Daniel H Pink addresses the need for more humanity in business with his view: 'Anytime you're tempted to upsell someone else, stop what you're doing and upserve instead.'[22] With the internet closing the information access gap, it is those firms who adopt an honest, fair and transparent service-focused strategy and employ individuals who can use emotional not just intellectual skills who will be able to work with new technology and continue to thrive.

With any business mission and vision you need to take people along with you, which (from my experience) can be one of the hardest things to do. Either consciously or subconsciously, everyone tends to be asking themselves the question: 'What's in it for me?'

Let's face it: without a team your business will undoubtedly fail or, at the least, face a difficult start, and emotion and cognitive bias play a huge role. You need to identify the 'imposter in the room' – unconscious bias – early and develop strategy, systems, controls and operations to move forward together on the right track; in other words, your team and business are aligned skilfully and emotionally to your target market needs.

Emotional intelligence and your business

What we now know to be called emotional intelligence (emotional quotient or EQ) is a concept originally coined by psychologists John Mayer and Peter Salovey and made famous by Daniel Goleman in his book, *Emotional Intelligence: Why it can matter more than IQ*.[23] Leadership and business success (it was thought) were down to the intelligence of individuals alone, something set by your genes or due to experience. With emotion as a main protagonist in the boardroom or shop floor of any business, we began to understand a different, more radical, notion: by using a range of scientific tools and techniques, we could not only manage our own internal and external emotional states, but also others' too.

EQ has now become a mainstay in staff training and coaching across all industries. In our approach to culture coding, it takes centre stage in providing a framework for keeping our staff, teams and customers aligned and in tune. EQ can also help us manage our own and others' mental health and wellbeing, which has been shown to be one of the most important factors in highly successful businesses.

In his book, Goleman divides emotional intelligence into personal and social competence, with five key areas between them:

Personal competence	Social competence
1. Self-awareness – moods, emotions	4. Empathy – awareness of others' feelings
2. Self-regulation – controlling impulses	5. Social skills – proficiency in managing relations
3. Motivation – passion, optimism, initiative	

Put simply, EQ is the ability to recognise your own feelings and those of others, to manage these emotions and to motivate yourself. Why is it important to the culture of your business?

According to research conducted by the recruitment agency the Hay Group, more than 50%

of employees lack motivation to keep learning and improving, 40% of people cannot work co-operatively (come on, we all have worked with these types) and 70% of all change initiatives fail because of people-based issues (poor leadership, teamwork and so on).[24]

Many organisations suffer from what is called the 'Peter Principle': psychologist Laurence J Peter's research found that people are generally promoted to their level of incompetence, meaning they tend to be picked for a position based on abilities relevant to their current rather than intended role.[25] I'm sure we've all wondered from time to time why certain people have gained their roles and responsibilities, and it's generally down to promotion based on technical expertise or social 'schmoozing' rather than blending in people skills. We all know the technical expert or social lounge lizard who makes for a poor boss.

It is those who are emotionally aware and recognise which emotions they are feeling, are aware of the connection between feelings, thoughts and actions and recognise this in others, and understand how these feelings and actions affect their own and others' performance, who will establish a healthy business environment.

When biases come into play, we suffer primary emotional impulses, and this is where (if we're not careful) we undo all the good work we have put into identifying, mapping and monitoring the desired behaviours and subsequent constructive culture that arises over time. If we give bias a free rein, we can move straight through into the blame game, negative internal dialogue or unrealistic expectations.

It is the same with technology and its application to business products and services. We have all heard the horror stories where moving to new technology platforms or introducing new technology has caused serious problems. You only have to look at the British Bank TSB, which made the headlines for all the wrong reasons with its cataclysmic IT migration failure in 2018. The company went live too soon with poor piloting and road-mapping work, principally due to a biased rule of thumb where the live date was based on assumptions driven by past projects undertaken by the third party SABIS – the technology organisation of the Spanish bank who had bought part of Lloyds TSB.

Suffice to say the project did not go well, locking TSB customers out of their online accounts for an extensive period. The company subsequently lost 880,000 customers and £330 million and its CEO was forced to resign. If a careful and detailed technology implementation plan had been designed in the first place by a diversified team of specialists using a research and design technology framework similar to the one I describe in Chapter One, then any board would have understood the third-party capabilities to deliver, what realistic time frames should have been, the audit and governance processes required and so on.

When you implement an EQ framework into your staff recruitment, learning and development policies and procedures, and your IT development programmes, don't discount the effects of bias and noise, which can create havoc if left unattended and mismanaged.

Culture carriers and the social business

A culture carrier is someone with intimate knowledge of the company values who employs their EQ to engage with others and understand why the company behaves the way it does. They become ambassadors for their company and passionately promote those values in their day-to-day dealings with clients and co-workers.

Essentially, culture carriers glue the culture to the organisational framework. The advantage of developing such individuals is they normally have high EQ and can scale the desired culture across the business at relatively low cost. By employing culture carriers you will be creating your own communications network within the business, which can be leveraged outside the business with client service, for example.

Just think for a moment about the benefits of having many people within your business amplifying the message you want to get across to all staff, management, the C-suite, stakeholders and your clients. You will generate what can be called a social business. This means that firms adopt social technology, media and networking so they can encourage behavioural standards across the business areas and engage with external audiences, including clients, prospects, recruits, suppliers and stakeholders.

What is imperative here is that you employ and engage with individuals within the business who demonstrate positive EQ. You can design and implement fancy social media and social enterprise technology that allows your communications to flow and engages your staff and clients, but without empathy, you face the high risk that all the good work you have put into ensuring your corporate culture is constructive will be undone quickly.

Developing emotional intelligence

It should now be clear that EQ can act as an agent for change in your business culture. If developed carefully across the business departments, EQ will act as a 'meta-analysis' tool so you can assess whether you have the right individuals in the right roles with the right skills within your business and make sure your clients' needs are continuously listened to and served. Then you can guard against behavioural challenges such as:

- **Emotional contagion:** This is a phenomenon where one person's emotional reactions are triggered in others implicitly or explicitly.

- **Emotionally laden judgements:** These are usually emotionally driven views on the state of the relationship between employer and employee – for example (un)appreciated, (dis) trusted, (under)valued.

- **Low-performing teams:** This is tied in to both of the above. If the culture supports negative emotional development, this will undoubtedly lead to poor performance of some kind, such as lack of buy-in to business goals or objectives or no accountability to the job and activities at hand.

- **Mistrust:** This is a big one and again a direct result of the top two points above. Negative emotions creating dysfunctional decision-making will lead to high risk and low trust within and outside the business. Let's face it, your customers or clients will be royally hacked off if your relationship management team do not respond to their needs effectively or efficiently.

If there is a direct link between emotions and culture, this begs the question: how can you build strategy to ensure you have EQ embedded across your business and thus your culture benefits?

A good place to start is recognising the existing emotions people within the organisation are feeling. This can be done in several ways: through one-to-one or team meetings, using psychometric tests or by enterprise social technology such as collaborative platforms allowing staff to explore their and others' thoughts.

If we return to Chapter Two, which discussed what determines organisational culture, then we see that, along with policies, procedures, systems and controls – ie the hard structure of the business – we have the soft facts that cover people's preferences, beliefs, habits and values. If you have the infrastructure and framework right, then you must also ensure you have the right people with the right EQ so they can carry the culture with them through the firm. You need them to become culture carriers.

Creating the right framework within your businesses to code the right culture means you must have the right people to build it in the first place. The problem with the current commercial system is that if you have the wrong people with the wrong skills and an infrastructure geared to the wrong metrics (remuneration based on product sales not client engagement, poor complaints handling and training), then any systems and controls will serve for a dysfunctional operation.

There are many examples here: the banking sector and the financial crises in 2008–2009, big technology refusing to buy start-ups only to be quickly surpassed, and accounting firms failing to conduct true governance and due diligence, leading to enormous losses. I could go on.

The point here is simple: without the right people with high EQ, you end up with a lopsided model that causes poor risk management, dysfunctional behaviour, disgruntled clients and staff and much worse. The driving force for your business success will always be your people – and aligning their decisions and activities with your business strategy and objectives. It is imperative, with EQ in mind, that we look at human resource development (HRD).

Human resource development

We cover HRD in more detail in Chapter Seven, but with EQ it is important to cover the essentials and spend a little time introducing the key issues.

Recruitment

When I studied for an MSc in organisational psychology (behaviour), the module that I always struggled with was recruitment. Why? It is so subjective and hard to get right. My own bias was playing games with my mind, as I had never really thought of myself as a human resources expert. When working in the wealth management industry in South East Asia, I always found it difficult to know if we had hired the right people until they were out in the field. This may be the same for many industries, but with EQ showing its prevalence as an indicator for functional and constructive behaviour, we now have a barometer we can use to ensure that the right people are hired.

Training and competence, learning and development

Again, those who emit good EQ stand a good chance of being open to training and learning programmes designed to ensure the right competence and conduct, and they can then apply their learning to their jobs. Those with IQ may fare well in the more transactional training and competence arena, where the focus can be on technical skills, but EQ is required for a more holistic performance across the hard and soft skills required in modern-day business.

Work and wellbeing

Now this is where I really struggled in my MSc. I was never involved with the HRD arena when working in wealth management; all I was interested in was keeping my and my wealth management team's private clients happy. Essentially, this is where EQ comes into its own both from an employee and employer perspective, plus it's all about empathy, something my wife says can be in short supply where I'm concerned! There are two areas for focus:

1. **Moods and emotions:** These are specific and thus we can be more accurate in managing and improving them. Moods can endure for a longer term, tend to be gradual and continuous in onset, are relatively intense, are not caused by a specific event and provide information about the state of the self. Emotions are relatively short-term, episodic and phasic; they can be relatively weak to strong in intensity, are caused by a specific event and provide information about the state of the situation.

2. **Stress and satisfaction:** These are crude ways of assessing feelings at work and addressing work and wellbeing issues.

Some behavioural scientists argue that stress doesn't really exist; that it is a vague explanation for a variety of anxiety-related issues and manifestations. To prioritise staff happiness, you need a framework to work with so you can monitor their wellbeing at work. Moods and emotions have five components:

1. Cognition (eg appraisal, evaluation)

2. Internal reaction (eg heart rate)

3. Overt behaviour (eg approach, avoidance)

4. Facial expression (eg frown, smile)

5. A goal structure (eg loss, happiness)

You need to be aware of what matters to people, and how their moods and emotions are affected by changes you make to key issues such as strategy, business systems or remuneration. EQ can help employers place their staff's and clients' wellbeing at the centre of their business infrastructure and strategy. Empathy ensures that employees feel safe and confident they are being treated fairly, and employers will have a framework to manage their staff's wellbeing effectively and for the good of their employees and their ongoing business objectives.

Interconnection between the brain and heart

There are two types of knowledge: articulate (the head), which is rational, practical and employs common sense, and tacit (the heart), which is emotional, experience-related and impulsive. This is important when we focus on culture coding, due to the fact that our staff and clients are people and employ both types of knowledge in their decision-making processes. We need to blend the two in the way we engage staff and clients to maintain our competitive advantage.

This, of course, involves demonstrating high EQ and, in particular, empathy to ensure we employ a blended approach and eliminate any biases. Historically, business has focused on articulate or learned knowledge rather than the more heart-centred implicit approach that tacit knowledge allows. As we have seen, people act from instinct, and we need to position our products and services in a way that ensures they make the best possible decision for their needs.

The key issue here is how you design and deliver your services, which is obviously based on how they will be received and perceived by customers and clients. You need to segment your clients by preferences and beliefs, which are generally driven by tacit knowledge. We will focus on this in more depth in Chapter Six but it's worth noting that aiming your business offerings at and delivering them to your customers' needs requires careful planning and incorporating experiential needs, an approach that will drive your competitive advantage. A culture that encourages a relational economy, one that respects that buyer behaviour is driven by both tacit and articulate knowledge, will drive a sustainable business practice through both positive and negative market conditions.

Emotional intelligence, technology and AI

There is no doubt that technology applied well (post the right research and due diligence process) to any business model acts as an enabler platform to streamline business practice and make systems, controls and services more effective and efficient. We cannot ignore this when discussing how we fine-tune our businesses so we have the best chance of success.

EQ plays an important role when applying technology to our businesses. This is because, at its heart, technology is human. It is built by humans generally for humans plus, most importantly, it is not magic. Having built technology for business, I know that all too well.

If any of you reading this book are parents, you will know how difficult it can be to keep children off their smartphones or tablets. It has been argued that technology can undermine social interaction and EQ along with it. If we know this up front, we can design the technology that we employ within our businesses and private lives around understanding how it can support constructive behaviour and connect our business, staff and our clients. What part does EQ play here?

When applying technology to business, you need to be completely in tune with what your people's and clients' wellbeing needs are and also how information and data can be used ethically to enhance performance. Those firms who are large enough to employ a chief information officer (CIO) will no doubt ensure that individual has an abundance of EQ. This is because they need to balance and blend the human and technology factors, making sure that technology:

- Dovetails with the emotional needs of staff and clients

- Is easy to use – intuitive, turnkey technology is of paramount importance

- Is designed around the business model, client needs and the brand

- Is flexible and upgrades are available to align with an agile business strategy

A while back there was a fashionable acronym (yes, another one) that was used when it came to employing technology within the business – SMAC – which stands for:

- **Social:** Includes a business's social media presence, incorporating interfaces and schedules.

- **Mobile:** Serves as the blanket name for all smart technologies that access the internet and are handheld, including phones, tablets and watches.

- **Analytics:** Produces results and feedback from large amounts of information. In our world of big data, analytics help make sense of reams of information by analysing data or social stats provided by the customer.

- **Cloud:** Serves as an internet platform. At this point, we're all familiar with the cloud, but for definition's sake, the cloud is a philosophy viewing the internet not only as a source of information but as a platform with which to build speedy digital apps and websites.

The key here is the fact that SMAC doesn't offer a full solution and is fairly generalist in its approach. There are many issues you need to take into account when applying technology to your business. Where EQ can help is ensuring technology addresses emotional needs and also keeps your staff and clients engaged. Two areas we will explore are:

1. **Enterprise social networking (ESN) technology:** This is a platform whose sole purpose is to help employees connect and communicate across the organisation. This can encourage learning and sharing ideas and identify pockets of knowledge that can be leveraged and deployed effectively.

2. **Gamification:** As we will see in the next chapter, this is the application of game-playing features and benefits, such as point scores and

competition, to encourage engagement with products or services.

The point here is that technology built around business strategy that incorporates empathy, the most important factor in EQ, can offer positive leverage to communications, services, systems and controls, MI and much more so that any business has streamlined its operational framework around the needs of its people and clients.

When it comes to AI, we have an interesting conundrum. There is no doubt AI is a major disrupter, and there are many consultants out there predicting jobs are at risk of being replaced by AI. An example list could be telemarketers, bookkeepers, compensation and benefits managers, receptionists, couriers, proofreaders, computer support specialists, market research analysts, advertising salespeople and retail salespeople.

There are also jobs that currently could not be replaced by AI: human resource managers, teachers, sportspeople, judges and lawyers, writers, chief executive officers, event planners, politicians, psychiatrists and psychologists, and surgeons.

You may see each occupation in the latter list requires high EQ and empathy along with IQ. There is also the fact that AI has limitations: it has been shown to be biased (yes, it's built by humans) and people just will not accept robots in some professions because of the risks involved in AI.

There is no doubt that there are lots of things machines can do better than humans: gathering and analysing data, interpreting the results, determining a recommended course of action, and implementing a course of action.

For example, doctors perform tests, analyse results, interpret results and make a diagnosis then plan a treatment course. Financial advisers conduct fact finds to gather and analyse data about their clients' needs and their investments; they then interpret the implications for risk tolerance and the capacity for loss, and plot and implement an investment strategy which is reviewed over time. Business consultants do much the same in helping firms implement their strategy.

AI can quickly surpass human capabilities in the first areas: data gathering and analysis. Where culture comes in is in humans' ability to adapt. Being the eternal optimist, the way I see it is this brings opportunity for AI to take over the more administrative tasks, allowing humans to apply their EQ to the interpretation of results – determining and implementing action.

If the culture we have built over time allows free thinking, challenge and change, then we have an adaptable framework that will encourage investment in the right technology. AI will then enhance human performance as humans will be free to focus on and refine their strength areas, using discretion, empathy and strategy based on the machine data outputs.

Some people may say that we will never trust machines with important decisions, such as the management of our health and money, but this is twentieth-century thinking. A new generation is now engaging with smart machines that they trust, and often prefer. It's hard for anyone to argue with the results. IBM's Watson is already cracking medical cases that stump doctors, and investors are fleeing expensive, actively managed funds for better-performing passive ones. The value of some of our most prized career paths is already being eroded.

Those that want to stay relevant in their professions will need to focus on skills and capabilities that AI has trouble replicating – understanding, motivating and interacting with human beings. A smart machine might be able to diagnose an illness and even recommend treatment better than a doctor. It takes a person, however, to sit with a patient, understand their life situation (finances, family, quality of life etc) and help determine what treatment plan is optimal. This means EQ is front and centre, as it's currently not possible for machines to replicate human intuition effectively or to replicate soft skills that are so relevant to gaining and maintaining human trust.

Those in the C-suite and in positions of influence within the business should nurture and invest in EQ in the same way they do with the technical skills required across roles within the business; this can effectively act as a safety net to prevent individuals from getting overwhelmed or feeling threatened if you decide to invest in technology and AI. It is an emotive issue, and if you show that you are continuing to invest and believe in your people as you build out your business infrastructure, your culture and climate within the business will be one of nurture and support for constructive change.

Chapter checkpoints

- Apply EQ as a 'meta-analysis' tool, so you can assess whether you have the right individuals on the right roles within your business and your clients' needs are continuously listened to and served.

- Nurture and invest in EQ in the same way you do with the technical skills required across roles within the business. This can effectively act as a safety net to ensure individuals do not get overwhelmed or feel threatened if you decide to invest in technology and AI.

- Use EQ to help you apply technology appropriately to the business and ensure you have the right people with the right skills deploying technology, and clients are well served.

FOUR
Gamification

W hen I started my regtech business, I knew that
my colleagues and I had to engage the world
of governance, risk and compliance (GRC) in a new
and different guise. This is because for many years
the financial services compliance industry has been
paper- and people-driven, using spreadsheets, checklists and tick boxes. Compliance professionals tend to
use disparate solutions to manage their GRC requirements, which can work well but also risk driving
misinformation and misunderstandings.

It was clear that compliance activities (particularly
audits) could benefit significantly from the application
of carefully designed technology. The challenge is that
the industry has worked in one way for so long, compliance professionals are (you guessed it) conservative
and this area is sensitive and granular by definition.

I decided to look to behavioural science and gamification to help create a new digitised platform that would provide a GRC hub: automating GRC diagnostics, gap analysis and audit activities; bringing compliance and business teams together; gaining real-time data and MI on compliance activities and behaviours, and real-time alerts on all regulatory risks; and providing a holistic solution which identified trend analysis in how all the relevant regulations relate to each other and to the business operations.

Gamification is the application of certain elements of game playing, such as point scoring, competition with others and rules of play, which can make mundane and difficult tasks far more engaging and rewarding. It can also employ the IKEA effect, in that those scoring well, gaining good quality data and MI on their audit activities and tracking positive improvements and results can heighten GRC engagement and provide excellent evidence that compliance teams are scoring consistently well against their regulatory performance requirements.

This means that compliance professionals can gain evidence that they are improving compliance scores against key regulatory areas – alerts that provide gap analysis, compliance diary integration and action tracking to evidence audit compliance – and that the team are all on the same page, gaining the same information across their heatmap dashboards, and can see how they are performing against their peers in the marketplace.

Gamification in business uses the principles of human behavioural psychology, such as our inherent desire to achieve competence, social relatedness and control of our professional lives, to drive intrinsic motivation and engagement. In our world, it allows firms to embrace a more constructive compliance culture, where technology is designed to motivate people into action, providing them with real-time data and leading to a more time- and cost-effective GRC management service and culture within the business.

One of the first things we did in my business was recruit a team of 'gamer' app developers who had nothing to do with retail financial services or compliance. This was important to ensure that our vision for enhancing engagement and consistency while reducing time and costs was possible, using technology as an enabler tool.

The system uses techniques such as:

- **Scoring rewards:** Individuals answer GRC questions across a number of relevant regulatory areas, gain GRC scores – with the algorithm providing 'dynamic steers' – and resources are allocated based on those scores to aid improvements where necessary.

- **GRC missions:** Actions are provided based on automated gap analysis and action tracking designed to ensure individuals engage in performing and recording the desired actions and behaviours that improve their scores.

- **Social proofing:** Individuals are scored against their peers in a way that fosters healthy competition and drive to mastery and competence on different topics inherent in the regulatory framework in which they work.

The results speak for themselves

Over a period, the results of integrating gamification indicate that firms are not only becoming more engaged with their GRC activities, but also saving audit time and costs to the tune of 30%. The software can also help reduce professional indemnity costs and identify tailored training and competence requirements for individuals, thus enhancing professional development, bringing better-designed systems and controls and reducing residual and inherent GRC risks.

There are a number of other gamification strategies organisations can employ to encourage positive behaviour. Take e-learning training and development programmes: they can employ gamification strategies to take the application of training in the workplace to another level. Other strategies include:

- **Right answers gain rewards:** Awarding points for each correct response can give participants quantifiable evidence of their progress. Many retail apps use this principle by offering more rewards based on purchases. Keeping score plays into human nature; people naturally become interested in an activity when there is something at stake, raising their sense of engagement on an emotional level and creating a visceral and positive experience.

- **Leader boards:** Used positively and ethically, leader boards can build a sense of community and friendly rivalry. Again with e-learning and training in mind, building a healthy competitive spirit across employees can help support a constructive culture and the aspiration to meet ongoing goals and objectives.

- **Levelling up:** Nothing to do with politics, this is all about providing new levels of learning once a level has been completed. It's the same with the compliance scoring we use in our regtech: once you reach a certain point, you move up a level to access new rewards and knowledge resources.

- **Personalisation:** The NRE helps employees relate to the activities and tasks they are being asked to do. Where e-learning is concerned, some participants may engage more if the software does not gamify everything or respond better in a scenario-based learning environment that relates to their everyday tasks.

- **Scenario testing:** Building on personalisation, if employees need training on a key regulatory directive such as operational resilience, then design a live stress test that encourages engagement with challenges that may actually arise across important business services (CRM platforms, telecommunications, IT systems). This activity can be further gamified by introducing a points system for every challenge solved.

In the context of customer engagement, many examples abound. Banks offer their customers rewards for using their credit or debit cards or the chance to set savings goals. Travel websites use gamification to encourage customer engagement so that those customers stick with them when booking their holidays. The healthcare industry employs gamification to encourage patient engagement with maintaining good health; for example, health insurers might provide social benefits such as gym membership or Fitbit discounts.

In my industry, there is no better example of the benefits of gamification for technology use to enhance client engagement and business profitability than financial advisers, planners and wealth managers. They use tools such as attitude to risk and cash flow modelling that work through a client's relationship with their savings and investments from a risk perspective and offers scenario testing, where certain circumstances can be stress-tested artificially so clients can view their financial data based on growth rates, charging structures, inflation rates and modelled life events such as health issues, death or marriage, education and retirement plans. Not only does this engage clients in their financial matters and make the firm more effective, dynamic and efficient in its client services, but it also encourages 'ownership' via endowment theory.

Algorithms and nudging your clients

Remember the IKEA effect – using endowment theory so individuals value your products or services far more because they have psychologically invested in them? This, along with loss aversion, means that if they have scored themselves on a credit score system such as ClearScore, they will want to improve their scores and will fret if their scores worsen over time.

If you think about social media technologies, they all have features that make them easy and engaging to use. If it's a like button, trending analysis, scoring, points and rewards or instant messaging, then users tend to gain instant gratification and want to continue using the software. This means that integrating such features into your service proposition(s) can be helpful in gaining what we call 'sticky' customer relationships over time.

Some examples of businesses gamifying their services include:

- **Omnicare:** They are America's largest provider of pharmacy services for long-term care facilities. Given the company's poor help desk results, with long wait times and high abandonment rates, they sought to gamify their customer service procedures by introducing employee points and rewards, and leader boards to motivate customer-facing staff.

- **EE:** The UK's largest mobile network operator required a new training platform to improve their staff's digital skills and compliance performance. They installed The Digital Academy, a social and gamified learning portal that provides learners with micro-courses using game-based quizzes to test knowledge, with badges, levels and leader boards available for further engagement and knowledge transfer.

- **HP:** One of the biggest technology brands partnered with Growth Engineering to create a mobile app, The HP Uni App, the purpose of which was to train sales teams on cybersecurity topics. The app used gamification to maximise learner engagement, encouraging learners to compete in a league format for the HP Security Cup. The results were impressive: the high levels of knowledge about cyber risks among sales staff brought a more competent sales and service function.

The key here is alignment between all stakeholders in the service proposition. Staff, and service and product providers need to agree on the best approach to meeting customer needs and objectives. Many businesses are slow on the uptake when it comes to gamifying their service proposition. This is hard to understand when you can evidence the results easily with the data and MI the technology provides.

Data analytics can ensure you have all the relevant information to hand to offer your staff the right training and development programmes for them to transfer learning to their activities and tasks, making sure they are competent and show exemplary conduct when engaging customers and services, and products are distributed in the right way to meet customer needs.

Bias and emotional intelligence

Such gamified technologies can also help manage biases and promote EQ through increased staff self-awareness and encouraging the culture to grow in a constructive way. As we have seen, there is no doubt AI will become a major player over time. You only have to look at the innovation within the automotive market to see car engineering companies using AI to market their new hybrid car and technology giants, focusing on driverless cars (still a way to go). This, along with AI technology used in self-prescription within healthcare, means there is an inevitability about the whole thing. What's the risk?

Well firstly we need to focus on what we currently have. As we know, good technology acts as an enabler and algorithms can provide meaningful data to aid decision-making, reduce noise and manage biases.

With the need for face-to-face interactions, there is also the issue of intuition, or, as psychologist Herbert Simon puts it, recognition. He writes: 'The situation has provided a cue; this cue has given the expert access to information stored in memory, and the information provides the answer. Intuition is nothing more and nothing less than recognition.'[26] This sense, or recognition based on previous experience (otherwise known as heuristics), can skew actions. There is evidence that customer relationship managers, for example, transpose their biases onto the client recommendations they provide.

What we humans and industry experts also have to contend with is will depletion. We get tired throughout the day, which means lack of energy can have a detrimental effect on decisions and actions.

Who's the winner? Although algorithms have the upper hand on emotion not getting in the way, presently they are only as good as the emotive human beings who built them. The variety of systems, controls, algorithms and technologies that can be used to better manage human behaviour, gain better results and promote a constructive culture, along with product and service segmentation, mean customers gain a personalised approach designed to meet their ongoing needs – a strategy that is highly desirable in the NRE.

Marginal gains

Sports science has always been ahead of the game in applying technology to improve performance. You probably have not heard of Wilhelm Steinitz, but it was his approach to developing a scientific method for his chess playing skills that led to him becoming the first chess world champion in 1886. Wilhelm's success lay in what has become known as the 'accumulation theory', or the accumulation of small advantages, which, in Wilhelm's case, was the ability to analyse and understand the position of the chess pieces to stay one step ahead of his opponents.

You only have to look at the England rugby team, who won the World Cup in 2003. Sir Clive Woodward applied 'critical, non-essentials', small things in everyday team preparations and activities to set them up ahead of their opponents.[27] When Team GB's Olympic cycling team won eight gold medals in 2012, Dave Brailsford, the British cycling performance director, explained: 'If you can break everything down that goes into riding a bike and improve it by 1%, you will get a significant increase when you put them together.'[28]

Marginal gains can be assessed by technology, using data on performance and pinpointing issues that can be improved. In the context of gamification, this means that if an individual or business values their data and performance, they will be heavily invested in improving it. The marginal gains approach dovetails with gamification to produce a powerful force for sustainable performance.

Chapter checkpoints

• Engage research technology that can offer gamification in a sophisticated fashion to ensure staff and clients gain value and are not disengaged by tools that may come across as too simplistic or be viewed as manipulative.

- Communicate clearly why you use gamification so that staff and clients understand and 'buy in' to using the technology and gamification features and benefits.

- Measure the data gamification produces. As with EBP, technology and gamification can provide high-quality data and MI so firms can understand staff and client needs, along with any gaps, and design solutions to meet them.

- Apply a marginal gains strategy to everyday activities and use technology to measure the issues for improvement prior to and post any intervention so you can assess the improvements and how they can be sustained.

PART TWO

THE FIVE CULTURE CODE KEYS

FIVE

Your Focus

Focus is the first of the culture code keys I set out in the introduction to this book. This key is all about strategic planning and marshalling the resources of the business so that goals and objectives are met and sustained. This is not to be confused with business planning, which is just a tour of the business operations.

The focus is on how strategic your thinking has been in planning for the future, incorporating GRC and leveraging internal and external resources to ensure you gain momentum fast and your culture is developing in the right way as you build.

The principle that applies across these five culture code keys and a business's operating system is that we apply EQ and its empathy strategy at the heart of all we do when planning and implementing technology and building our culture coding framework. If we do not do this, then we can fall into the trap of behaviour driven by ego and bias, which leads to navel-gazing, poor communications and a failing culture. By employing empathy at an early stage, we can holistically monitor all actors in play, so we then identify, manage and monitor such risk and place the more dysfunctional emotions to one side as we build and implement our culture code.

Evidence-based practice

One approach that can help business professionals when building their business model is to apply critical thinking to their role and the way it interrelates with the business. Taking a step back and using diagnostic tools can promote the move from 'Do we think this is true?' to 'We know this is true.'

In the world of social science this is known as evidence-based practice and I am placing this first and foremost in this chapter because, in commercial life, we need to be certain our business strategy and the culture that is subsequently developed is based on hard and soft facts.

> **EVIDENCE-BASED PRACTICE**
> - Learning about cause–effect connections in professional practices
> - Isolating the variations that measurably affect desired outcomes

- Creating a culture of evidence-based decision-making and research participation
- Using information-sharing communities to reduce overuse, underuse and misuse of specific practices
- Building decision supports to promote practices that the evidence validates, along with techniques and artefacts that make the decision easier to execute or perform (eg checklists and protocols)
- Having individual, organisational and institutional factors that promote access to knowledge and its use[29]

As I wrote in my book *Winning Client Trust*, as an analogy: if we still believed the world was flat and based our everyday planning around this assumption, the world would be a different place than it is today.[30] As Columbus found, we need to explore to find evidence to provide better knowledge to understand exactly what any landscape may look like.[31] This applies to MI and the marketplace into which we want to launch our business. We need to know our markets intimately, then choose a target market so we can effectively gain a niche market to where we aim our service offering(s).

In management speak (something I like to avoid) this is called identifying a gap in the market and a market in the gap. Developing the right strategy is probably the most important step, as this sets the tone and mood music for the subsequent culture and climate to develop over time and enable us to employ the right technology to serve our business and client needs. What's the best way to start planning strategically and ensure the right culture is developed over time?

It is important to break down the strategic planning into 'bite-sized chunks'. I would recommend you focus on four constituent parts:

1. The most important part is writing a bona fide strategic plan based on EBP. This might sound obvious but without a plan in place we have no real direction in which to head.

2. Next is organisational engagement: this includes good communication channels to make sure everyone fully understands the message, the plan and what you are trying to achieve.

3. Strategic differentiation entails mapping how different we are from potential competitors in the market(s) we have chosen to compete in, and working out what differentiates your service or product offering(s) so prospective customers or clients can clearly see the value you are offering them.

4. Finally, agility. How flexible the business is in meeting changing technology trends, opportunities and challenges is important, as this can make the difference for determining the long-term success and sustainability of the business.

The new relationship economy

The client is king. Well yes and no. As we'll see in Chapter Seven, ensuring you have the right people in your business is just as important as keeping your customers: the common denominator is relationships and behaviour. The NRE means the move – via key market drivers such as government policy, regulation, products and services – to service and product personalisation. In other words, personalisation is key. There are a variety of issues at play here:

- Organisations are ecosystems.

- Clients matter more than competitors.

- Markets and competitors are dynamic.

- Strategy is about choice.

- Big is not always best.

- Corporate social development matters.

- High-touch technology is an enabler.

Organisations are ecosystems

This means a more holistic approach is required to understand the interconnected nature of modern business. The traditional linear model of suppliers and distributors is too simplistic. You need to have a grasp on ideas as your IP and not products; for instance, you can joint venture with competitors who may have a better product than yours, or partner with services.

Clients matter more than competitors

Insights, meaningful experience and intuitive personal products and services are now what matter most if you want to be relevant. Client-centricity has become the enduring pursuit of every business. Clients now expect subscription experiences with ongoing value – memorable experiences, immediate fulfilment, a service that is available any time, anywhere, and full of personalised moments. This links us with the first point – think social media or digital travel agencies, whose business model is not hard product, but experiential and relational.

Markets and competitors are dynamic

In connected and convergent markets boundaries blur and competitors can not only challenge physically but also virtually from any corner of the planet. The Covid-19 pandemic has taught us the importance of digital services and products in remote working. We have seen a boom in online conferencing – one particular conferencing platform made two years' worth of revenue in the first two months of lockdown. Again, you have to be mindful of the relational issues that affect people inside and outside your business.

Strategy is about choice

As we have seen, gaining the right strategy is a road map to the future growth of your business. It is also about developing your vision – ie your purpose, innovative mindset, and staff and customer experiences that will keep you on track. Porter's Five Forces model can be a good benchmark, it relies on finding a position in stable markets and, as we know, markets can be far from stable, so agility is key.[32]

Big is not always best

The assumption is that companies will win through scale. The term 'too big to fail' was certainly true for some of the banks during the 2008–2009 financial crises, yet today's winners succeed through better ideas and vision executed effectively and efficiently. This can mean partnering with larger firms to focus on niches of relevant customers and markets and staying small, smart and agile to manage risk.

Corporate social development

In a world that sits on the precipice when it comes to pollution, debt and poverty, the NRE means you can leverage the interconnected world for the better. With business taking a step back and engaging in social responsibility and social awareness, environmental, social and governance (ESG) criteria used by business, regulators and investors alike to screen investments for being green and socially responsible and to impact investing credentials means that the relationship between business outputs and the state of society has never been stronger or more under focus. Ellen MacArthur has conducted exemplary work on a circular economy[33] (recover and regenerate) as an alternative to a traditional linear economy (make, use, dispose).

High-touch technology

As we touched on in Chapter One, we are now well into the 4IR: that of digital innovation and all it brings. Discount technology at your peril. Although it is not magic (as I remind my clients), designed and built well it is a great enabler platform for firms to streamline and work more effectively and efficiently. Technology can facilitate strong team and client relationships, allow communications to be spread uniformly throughout an organisation, employ algorithms to scrutinise data for quality MI covering risk, governance and compliance analysis, and support expansion into new markets.

Assess the relational issues

The economy in which we now operate is highly relational at micro levels. We need to engage our clients and staff where it matters if we want to create long-term value for all stakeholders. If we look at the difficulties we face as a planet through the climate emergency, we can see how an interconnected global economy can cause great problems if left unchecked. If we use EQ and place social corporate development and relationship capital along with technology as an enabler at the heart of our business strategy using the seven areas outlined above, this will place us in a strong position to grow, partner, adapt and sustain performance through both good and tough market conditions.

This means when you are applying a culture code to your business, you should always assess the relational issues first and foremost. The five keys allow you to continually build a mutually reliant and balanced business that is respectful to all stakeholders in your markets and to move fast and effectively to maximise any opportunities that are identified.

Strategic planning and your vision

With EBP and NRE in mind, how can you make certain you have the right strategic plan and framework in place to encourage a constructive culture and a streamlined business model fine-tuned to your clients' needs and the markets in which you operate?

Firstly, if you're starting out, you will need to decide what is inside and what is outside your plan. This might sound simple, but determining what you want to focus on is important, as this will have a strong influence on how quickly you gain momentum and achieve the quick wins that are important for your confidence.

What should you include? It may be obvious, but you need to decide where you're starting. This will confirm everyone is on the same page and on board with the journey. It is essential businesses develop a mission statement. In his book *7 Habits of Highly Effective People*, Stephen Covey discusses aligning values with principles/objectives; if you have achieved this then you find your 'due north'.[34] This means including the five principles in your mission statement, combined with your people, processes and philosophy. The top tip for your mission statement is what I call your 'T-shirt test': if you printed your mission statement on a T-shirt would your staff and clients wear it? Your business needs to align with the NRE.

DEFINING YOUR MISSION STATEMENT

- Expresses your core purpose
- Aligns staff to objectives
- Outlines company and staff values
- Inspires and motivates
- Is practical and market-focused

Next, you need to know the information required to move forward, which effectively means gathering available data from, for example, the market(s) you are going to operate in, and establishing what stakeholders want and need: for example, customers, staff, regulators and government. This data can be collaborated using simple tools such as a strengths, weaknesses, opportunities and threats (SWOT) analysis, with strengths and weaknesses focused on internal issues and opportunities and threats on external issues. There are many other tools available, and one I particularly like is PESTLER, which I have adapted and will touch on later in this chapter; but there are big issues here, in that management schools, periodicals and their outputs, including theories on business success, can suffer from a bias I label as 'self-determination', which effectively pulls together biases such as halo bias and groupthink, where theories and strategies are based on lower validity and a lack of diverse research and/or skill sets.

One of my favourite business authors, Matthew Syed, argues in his latest book, *Rebel Ideas*,[35] that it is those organisations that can pull together a team made up of a diverse set of experience and skills that can make key breakthroughs and bring a creative mindset to different tasks. We know EQ has a part to play here in building empathy across teams and offering diverse skills so that the end goal or mission is kept in check and MI and data is scrutinised and analysed more effectively, building in challenge and lateral thinking.

When the data is assessed, you can build a more holistic track for your business journey, focused on where you want to end up – ie your vision for the business over a set time frame. I have outlined below four characteristics of a vision statement you might want to consider. The key to a successful vision statement is ensuring it is 'big and hairy'; in other words, it will blow the doors off and see you through challenging times.

> **DEFINING YOUR VISION STATEMENT**
> - Aligned with firm and staff values
> - Builds a creative culture
> - Clear and concise
> - Audacious

Along this track you need to build in measurable goals, which can be specific, measurable, accurate, realistic, time-bound, ecological and reviewed (SMARTER). These goals would normally fit within quarterly or monthly timescales.

You then need to build in objectives, or long-term aims, which can be split into five areas (they may look familiar, given our five culture code keys):

1. Business model/strategy

2. Client/stakeholder engagement

3. Service proposition

4. Systems and operations

5. People development

By setting out your objectives in this way you can then align your shorter-term goals to the keys, thus bringing together activity in a focused way so all staff are working to the same common long-term objectives. It is important to mention that goals are different to objectives as they can be varied and wide, whereas objectives, whether corporate or individual, should be focused and static. The goals can be measured through action planning, which can be structured across what you want to measure, your aims, tasks, resources, responsibilities and time frames.

Whether you are a start-up or an SME, your strategic plan should be focused on your short-, medium- and long-term aims and ensure your culture grows in a constructive way, and it should be sense-checked at regular intervals. Again, the important point here is that it does not matter if you are a new or mature business; you can apply these principles at any time and ensure you are on track to meet your targets.

In addressing strategy, mission and vision, business will do well to align with the NRE and ensure specific aspects meet the client needs and investor requirements for scalability.

By focusing on developing a constructive culture code, you will need the technology that acts as an enabler throughout the business. This means addressing all the other keys within your focus key to assess whether you have the right technology embedded across your business.

As Chapter One detailed, you need to find technology that can streamline information and provide quality data and MI along with offering efficiencies that will allow your business to scale fast to take advantage of the NRE. Here you'll need to focus on essential tenets across:

- Solving client challenges and seamlessly meeting their needs

- Ensuring all stakeholders are continuously on the same page

- Favouring accountability and transparency

- Working towards long-term impact

If you put the work in and develop a granular and strategic technology research and implementation plan, this will place your focus in a strong position to grow and succeed.

Building a resilient business

I started writing this book during the Covid-19 pandemic lockdown, so one of the key focus areas for a business now is plain survival. Building resilience is key to this and has become one of the most important factors within this culture code key. A heavy focus on building a resilient culture is part of the regulation in my industry. As we have seen, in building and maintaining a business strategy, mission, vision and motivational leadership are essential to any enterprise, but to truly separate winners from losers over the long term, building and maintaining enterprise resilience is crucial.

To be resilient, you need to be able to manage through a crisis or disruption to business as usual (we certainly are presently), but you also need to anticipate what is coming down the line and evolve to meet a changing landscape with confidence so you can capitalise on it. For example, at the moment our regtech business Model Office operates completely virtually, with our team working from home across the UK and internationally, but we are seeing the light bulb switching on across our target market as they understand the need to move to remote working and are thus looking at how technology can help their audit processes. Guess what? They can send in our technology rather than people and gain more MI and data.

Building a truly resilient culture comprises three traits:

1. **Coherence and agility:** As described in the section on developing your strategic plan, you need to ensure your communications, decision-making and ability to adapt are embedded in your corporate mindset. This involves having the right OSS technology and people in appropriate roles and a structure that everyone understands, and making sure operations and business functions are maintained and delivered to your clients, as well as being certain these operations can support recovery and revive a firm after a material shock that threatens viability. Plenty of examples abound here, particularly in the age of cyber risks, such as the WannaCry ransomware attacks that affected the NHS trusts and hospitals so badly in 2018.

2. **Relevance and reliability:** Tied in to your mission and vision statements, these traits

represent your firm's relationships with all stakeholders, and are equally important in your business's ability to respond to change and challenge. This area relies more on the soft skills than the hard structure of the business, so yes, you should bring in the EQ approach and be mindful of biases and dysfunctional behaviours at play that can derail resilient culture.

3. **EBP:** As we have seen, technology can help ensure you have quality data and MI to illustrate where gaps are and evidence action taken to enforce a resilient culture.

BUILDING A RESILIENT FRAMEWORK

- Risk management
- Cyber risks
- Technology
- Disaster recovery
- Business continuity
- Scenario analysis
- Outsourcing
- Incident management

Governance, risk and compliance

Resilience testing is required to ensure you maintain this culture through your journey. This means you need to focus on continuous improvements and key to this is a strong GRC framework.

We can focus on two areas here:

1. Showing competence across skills and operations will identify key issues and their root causes and define a response and resolution.

2. Embedding the right conduct across the enterprise will involve making sure your people have the skills to identify, monitor and manage risks, and the right tools to do so (training and development, technology), that the board have the right blended skills, as we have already discussed, and that any areas that can undermine good conduct (yes, human bias) are identified and managed. This could be overconfidence in processes resulting in poor complaints handling or remuneration strategy.

With both of the above in place, you will have significant lines of defence to ensure a culture of accountability with 'four-eyes' (a minimum of two people) sense checks and independent assurance.

Accountability is a core part of your focus key; without it, the gel that binds the business strategy, resilience, innovation and overall culture will evaporate quickly. Having a team that will take personal responsibility for tackling issues, and going above and beyond to support colleagues and clients or to resolve customer problems are highly desirable if you want accountability and responsibility within your business.

Returning to our strategy and EBP framework, accountability should be at the heart of the mission statement right at the start of your strategic process, and the SMARTER goal structure should be used to add KPIs by which outcomes can be measured. This keeps everyone on track and engaged with the goals and long-term objectives to achieve the desired results. As we will see in Chapter Seven, ensuring the right team is in place is probably the most important issue when considering culture coding; you can focus all you want on the strategy, customer engagement, service proposition or systems and controls, but without a tightknit team spirit, you won't get to where you need and want to be. It is imperative that you have the right team to ensure you have the right mission and vision, but also so you have properly assessed, monitored and managed risk.

Risk is the combination of impact (the potential harm that could be caused) and probability (the likelihood of the issue or event occurring), and you need to cover and continually assess all areas. This can be done in a multitude of ways. We have already reviewed the SWOT analysis, which can be used as a simplistic formula to review internal and external risks; another worth noting is the PESTLE formula, to which I have added the 'R' of regulation, given that most industries have to operate in regulated environments.[36]

This formula is used to review outside forces that can affect the business. The most important issue is that it can be adapted and is flexible in its usage across your external risk assessment.

THE PESTLE(R) FRAMEWORK

- **Political:** Government, policy, stability, corruption, taxation, trade, restrictions
- **Economic:** Growth, exchange rates, interest rates, inflation, income, unemployment
- **Social:** Population, demographics, career, attitudes, behaviour, health, lifestyle, culture
- **Technological:** Financial, incentives, innovation, research and development activity, awareness
- **Legal:** Discrimination, antitrust laws, consumer protection, copyright/patent, health and safety
- **Environmental:** Weather, climate, environmental, emergency, NGO pressure
- **Regulations:** Rules, directives, outcomes, governance, risk, compliance

---

Building sustainable business advantage

This NRE and demand for personalisation bring the need to go above and beyond. What I mean by this is that with a fast-moving, experiential, driven economy, we cannot rest on any laurels.

When it comes to the 4IR, we only have to cite what has become known as 'Moore's Law'.[37] Gordon Moore, the then chairman of Intel, proposed that the number of transistors on a chip doubles every eighteen months. This has held up over time, with computer chips now 500 times faster than they were when Intel introduced its first PC in 1981.

When considering digital solutions, and in particular AI, embracing the NRE means we stand a chance of staying one step ahead of the game by building a business infrastructure that produces instant data and real-time information, streamlined services that provide instant customer fulfilment, and personalised touches available anywhere and any time.

In their book *Beyond Great*, Bhattacharya, Lang and Hemerling argue that with economic nationalism (think Brexit), social tension and technological revolution has ripped up the traditional business rule book, which offered shareholder value in a stable economic system.[38] Firms now need to think in the following ways:

- **Grow beyond:** They embrace streaming and refine their game by ensuring they do good as well as make profits (think corporate social development).

- **Operate beyond:** They craft a sustainable business strategy by augmenting low-cost delivery with high speed and flexible delivery networks. Joint ventures and partnerships with other businesses also enable firms to quickly leverage structure, strategy and digital supply chains, collecting valuable data and MI along the way.

- **Organise beyond:** They are client-focused at all times throughout the business infrastructure, ensuring teams are agile and skilled with digital tools and capabilities and enabling flexible structures that can respond and adapt quickly to shifting environments.

This all means that a relational, digital-savvy business will always be ready, never unprepared to deliver highly personalised experiences for their clients and staff alike.

With a relational economy, we break the mould of more transactional models. Businesses and the market(s) in which they operate are effectively psychological contracts, and business strategy is built around perceived risks, targets and goals. This means that we need to take into account the behavioural biases and the havoc they could reap on all the good work the business has built.

The relational focus and agile nature this framework demands mean firms need to have a number of strategies in place (particularly in the post-pandemic 'new normal' we now find ourselves).

CASE STUDY: Model Office – MO® Governance, Risk and Compliance RegTech

Model Office have identified that there is a certain amount of compliance 'dead' time firms can cut from GRC activities, which will allow them to spend more quality time with ongoing client and business strategy needs. By applying our MO® regtech governance, risk and compliance audit software to automate the audit of client file reviews, the compliance of policy documents, audits and report writing, and to streamline regulatory reports, firms can currently save at least 30% of time and associated costs plus ensure they gain higher quality MI and data in real time.

This equates to up to three hours a week, or a month a year, firms can gain back to spend on business- and client-associated activities. Applied correctly, regtech can cut out compliance dead time across travel, onsite/virtual audit fact-finding, manual client files, compliance document reviews and audit report writing, presentation and related actions and strategy. As we can see in the figure below, depending on the retail intermediary adviser's (RIA's) business model, regtech can save 30–50% of time and associated compliance costs.

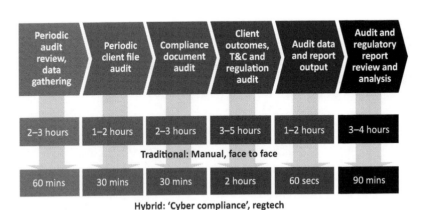

Periodic audit review, data gathering	Periodic client file audit	Compliance document audit	Client outcomes, T&C and regulation audit	Audit data and report output	Audit and regulatory report review and analysis
2–3 hours	1–2 hours	2–3 hours	3–5 hours	1–2 hours	3–4 hours

Traditional: Manual, face to face

| 60 mins | 30 mins | 30 mins | 2 hours | 60 secs | 90 mins |

Hybrid: 'Cyber compliance', regtech

Regtech and alleviated GRC dead time

Chapter checkpoints

- Make your corporate mantra: 'Design a flexible structure, do not rely too much on traditional business management tools and techniques, and question everything.' Employ EBP to ensure you have the evidence to make changes and tweaks to your business strategies.

- Ensure your technology uses OSS. This is important for two reasons: the NRE demands integration, outsourcing and innovative technology, and businesses and their clients need to ensure data and MI flows freely and securely.

- Employ a risk policy. This should be front and centre of every business decision and put the right structure in place to manage unknown unknowns.

- Focus on your people policy. Recruitment policy is essential to success, as we will see in Chapter Seven.

SIX
Your Engagement

A key component of culture coding is ensuring your product and service messaging and internal and external relationships are aligned. If they are not, this has serious ramifications for sustainable performance and also creates key risks across governance, compliance and trusted client and stakeholder relationships.

This key focuses on your business brand, your marketing strategy, how well your client documents are structured and how you develop deep, loyal and trusted relationships with clients and other stakeholders.

Aligned with the processes discussed in the next two chapters, your engagement strategies need to have systems and controls to give you the best possible opportunity to gain partner relationships with all stakeholders across the business. Only then will you gain a constructive culture for engaging the NRE in the right way.

If you use technology to manage destructive behaviours and help you filter out unhelpful bias and noise in your decision-making, then you stand a greater chance of getting the business where it needs to be in gaining trusted status across all stakeholders. As Sir Clive Woodward, England Rugby World Cup-winning manager, says, 'Business is no different to sport. Data and technology is a very powerful tool, but only if every individual in your team knows how and why they are using it.'[39] Applying technology is one thing, but we need to ensure our staff know how to use it and the data outputs it provides.

Algorithms can provide choice architecture to enable better decisions: they see and manage any bias and noise affecting their decisions and they can make better decisions for the good of the business, not just themselves.

Your reputation

When we look to buy a home, we are reminded of the estate agent mantra: 'Location, location, location.' When we address culture coding, the importance of relationship capital and the engagement of all stakeholders, it is all about reputation, reputation, reputation. We all know individuals who have spent years building their career or brand only for this to come undone in a matter of days, hours or minutes. You only have to look at the fragility of political careers to see this in action. As we have seen, with a focus on operational and financial resilience during and post the Covid-19 pandemic, a resilient reputation is something to be praised.

The problem here is, no matter how hard you have worked on the practicalities of building your focus across business planning, strategy and GRC management, if you take your finger off the culture pulse for an instant, your reputation can be terminally damaged.

This is invariably down to behavioural bias and a transactional rather than a relational focus when engaging clients and stakeholders and thinking about the important role relationship capital plays in bonding them to your business.

This requires high trust and developing an excellent reputation, both of which involve your people, but also are defined by how well you have designed your client journey map and stakeholder engagement strategy.

On the issue of retaining clients, David Maister's Trust Equation should be considered.[40] Built on the metric of adding credibility, reliability and intimacy and then dividing this by self-orientation, this equation depends on the strength and depth of relationship capital built with customers and clients and may be skewed by new relationships or those with poor personal chemistry. The key here is that all CEOs know that a lack of trust in business, both inside and outside the firm, is a massive threat to their growth prospects. Creating worthy investments and rewarding relationships is key.

> **THE TRUSTWORTHINESS EQUATION**
>
> $T = C + R + I \div S$
>
> T = Trustworthiness
>
> C = Credibility
>
> R = Reliability
>
> I = Intimacy
>
> S = Self-orientation

Remember the NRE and personalisation? Where reputation is concerned, you need to ensure your business and technology focus is aligned to your customers' needs and wants. This also means your brand and marketing strategies are built around the client journey. You need to attract the right clients and if you have a culture that is client-centric then this will bode well and create sticky relationships.

Reputation is based on your clients' experience and how they and prospective customers view your business. In this case, in terms of culture, you need to gain high levels of trust in your customer relationships, which is earned over time. One way to do this is to build a metric and measure relationship capital.

Relationship capital

As mentioned in Chapter Five, one of the most enduring equations to measure relationship capital is business consultant David Maister's trust equation. This is built on the premise that if we can keep our ego (and biases) at bay and focus on building deep, meaningful relationships with our clients, this will substantially increase our relationship capital and develop what I call trusted partner relationships.

With bias and noise in mind, if we have built strong customer relationship capital, then self-orientation is something we need to be mindful of. According to Maister, co-indicators of self-orientation could be a culture that encourages:

- Listing capabilities and qualifications

- Dropping names and relating stories to ourselves

- Not listening and appearing to be bright or clever

In other words, a self-interested culture means that customers will feel left out in the cold.

We need to be mindful of blending a deep, positive personal connection along with a business connection. As we can see in the figure below, trusted partner–customer relationships are found in those organisations who can ensure they gain a strategic approach to the customer journey and blend a highly personalised approach with services and products customers value. Their relationships will then remain top-right in customer perception and service and/or product engagement experience.

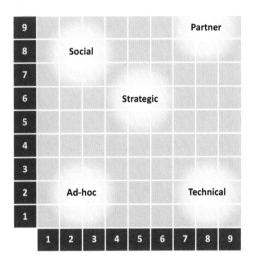

Relationship capital grid

A partner relationship is one with extremely high relationship capital and it is something worth measuring. If you are genuinely interested in improving your customer engagement, it is worth reading David Lambert and Keith Dugdale's book *Smarter Selling*.[41] Lambert and Dugdale assess the difference between goodwill, which accountants and solicitors tend to rely on, and the value of relationships.

Individually, relationship capital is essentially the value of one person's relationships; from an organisational perspective it is the sum of all the relationships within the business. This will include all stakeholders. It follows that if you develop strong networks, then you will generate high relationship capital scores.

A business that can generate strong relationship capital both internally and externally will have a positive and constructive culture in the engagement key. It then follows that business success, and indeed success in life generally, is highly dependent on relationships. Let's look at some strategies that can help generate high relationship capital and a positive cultural framework when it comes to engaging your customers.

Measuring your customer effort score

One of the most irritating and challenging issues I have faced when consulting with businesses is that they can overcomplicate the customer journey. Whether you are engaged in direct-to-client (D2C) or business-to-business (B2B) or even business-to-business-to-client (B2B2C), it does not matter when it comes to ensuring customer loyalty and trust; you need to make their journey relatively easy. This means you need to shift from surveying your customers from the perspective of a promoter to showing how easy you will make it for them if they do business with you.

As students of marketing well know, customer effort score (CES) is not a new concept but an interesting change in this dynamic, which started with an article in 2010.[42] A US consultancy conducted a study of more than 75,000 people who had interacted over the phone with contact-centre representatives or self-service channels (web, voice prompts, chat or email). They found two things: delighting customers doesn't build loyalty, reducing their effort does.

There are a variety of ways to manage customer satisfaction. Many businesses focus on surveying customers, and the CES is a metric used where customers rank their experience on a seven-point scale ranging from 'very difficult' to 'very easy'. This then determines how much effort was required to use the product or service and how likely it is they'll continue to pay for it. Notice the shift from satisfaction to experience. Customer loyalty is a true business driver in a competitive landscape and, as we have seen, the NRE effectively demands that we place a high focus on enhancing customer experience. Employing a system or team to gauge the ease of experience is paramount in encouraging a culture of trusted customer engagement.

It's worth spending a little time on how techniques and tools can give you the best chance of gaining a high CES and the benefits that brings. These might include the following:

- Most companies tend to employ a CES survey immediately after a touchpoint with customer service or after an important product or service engagement. That way, there is a better chance of a customer providing information, plus it makes sense as the survey is based on a recent experience. A net promoter score, for instance, tends to ask broad and fluid questions, such as: 'How likely is it you will recommend us to others?' A CES survey tends to be more focused and strikes while the iron is hot.

- Positive CES can indicate user-friendly and well-designed products and services. Negative responses alter your customer service and product management teams to create roadblocks in the customer experience. This provides a great opportunity: if you follow up a 'distressed' customer to learn about their engagement, you'll gain valuable feedback and potentially prevent losing them.

- A CES can be the strongest predictor of future purchase behaviour (a *Harvard Business Review* study indicates 94% customers with a high CES score would repurchase, while 88% would increase spending) and make referrals more likely (81% of customers who reported high effort said they would speak negatively). It is also highly actionable.[43]

- A CES can fail to provide information regarding a client's overall relationship with the business and demonstrates a lack of segmentation across client type.

- Some businesses use CES to measure the aggregate experience a customer or prospect has with their brand perception – EasyJet take note!

Joking aside, ascertaining how easy you make it for customers to engage with your products and services and how they see your brand is powerful and aligned to our NRE concept where experience is king, but it's not without its shortfalls. One of the key, and often underrated, issues in marketing and customer engagement is segmentation of your customers' needs and requirements.

Client segmentation and technology

Too many businesses adopt a scattergun strategy for marketing to and servicing their customers; or, if they do use segmented strategies, they focus on what I call the hard facts: for example, demographics, financial assets or KPIs. Many firms still use balanced score-cards and Porter's Five Forces strategies.[44] These approaches tend to be fairly static and dependent on functional markets, yet, again as the black swan event Covid-19 has shown, it's not that simple. If we are to understand our customers intimately and align our brand, product and services to their needs, this relationship economy we find ourselves in demands that we should segment customers by their behaviours.

This means factoring in the NRE framework and acknowledging customer buying behaviours and, yes, biases. When you focus on building EQ into your business strategies, this should be at the heart of how you engage your customers.

The table below illustrates an example from retail financial services where client segments can be driven by emotive issues. Some may not be proactive because they are driven by fear of lack of money and time, or because they are poorly organised. This means you need to take biases and behaviours into account when engaging customers with your services and products. If you can empathise, and identify the behavioural drivers, you can then deliver focused and tailored solutions to meet their individual needs.

Segmentation by behaviour in financial services

Segment	Behaviours	Financial needs and strategies to engage
Self-directed	Take financial decisions on their own, seek best products and prices	Information, value, speed, self-control
Validators	Interested in finances, seek advice on complex decisions	Tailored information, value, advice, reassurance, trusted relationships
Delegators	Bored or confused by finance, want others to take decisions for them	Personal planning, good service, coaching, trusted relationships
Avoiders	Neglect their finances, distrust firms, risk-averse	Simplicity, clear communications, ease of access

Along with focusing on EQ and the role of empathy here, we also need to look at the importance of relationships and relationship capital.

Whether you're involved in B2B or B2C, there are eight key principles you need to employ to ensure you're aligned with your customers' needs and developing strong relationship capital. They are:

1. Helpfulness

2. Value for time

3. Recognition

4. Promise fulfilment

5. Problem-solving

6. Personalisation

7. Competence

8. Accessibility

These eight points speak for themselves, yet we rarely witness them all in action at once when it comes to customer engagement. The key to this is focusing on the NRE and how technology can reduce customer effort. This is applicable to all channels within the business, resonates with staff and is generally low cost for everyone. If you're focusing on emotions and relationships and their importance to engaging your product and services, there are three areas you need to contemplate:

1. **Cognitive energy:** If you place too much information or jargon in front of your customers, ask them to remember too many passwords or consistently ask for card details; if customers are unable to get through your security system, your terms and conditions are longer than *War and Peace* or you constantly change account managers; if complaints procedures are not transparent or your website is difficult to navigate, this all means way too much pressure on customers' decision-making and brain power.

This is exemplified well by Daniel Kahneman's work on thinking fast and slow, as the table below shows.

2. **Emotional energy:** If staff have a poor attitude, are elusive, leave customers waiting or only engage when they want to sell something, this will lead to a build-up of negative emotions such as frustration and anxiety for your customers.

3. **Physical energy:** This can be queuing, travelling time or cold handovers where customers have to repeat their details – anything that involves your customers using up their time physically – and it can also be annoying.

Cognitive thinking through systems 1 and 2

	System 1	System 2
Characteristics	Effortless, triggers emotion, fast, unconscious, looks for causation, creates stories to make sense of events	Effortful, slow, logical, conscious, deliberate, handles abstract concepts
Advantages	Speed of response, easy completion of routine	Allows reflection and consideration, consequences, options, good at maths and stats
Disadvantages	Jumps to conclusions, unhelpful emotional responses, can make errors that are not detected or corrected	Slow so requires time, requires effort and energy, which can lead to decision fatigue

Put simply, if you're engaged in B2C then you need to employ a segmented balancing act to ensure your clients' energy levels are not worn out and wasted on useless and unhelpful messages. Instead, offer focused communications, reassurance, flexibility, simplicity and effortless engagement based around their known needs so they immediately see the personal benefits of purchasing your services.

If you are B2B, clients want to know quickly that you understand their business and that you listen and are responsive to their needs. A contact point, or 'gatekeeper', is always helpful in providing a personal and tailored approach. In other words, in both B2C and B2B client engagement, business needs to employ EQ, and empathy in particular, to build sustained relationship capital.

You will therefore want to employ turnkey technology that operates algorithms that make it incredibly easy for clients to engage in your products and services and gain instant information and gratification. Just look at website cookies, social media sites or cloud-based voice recognition services available on more than 100 million devices that track user behaviour: they all tailor products to user behaviour, so this may be an area that could improve your client engagement, and CES will ensure your technology is delivering this experience at all times.

If we look back to the CES and client satisfaction scoring, we can see that companies will create loyal customers by making it easy for them to become a customer and helping solve their problems quickly and easily.

What you need to do is focus on trust and relationship capital, making it personal and engaging but, most importantly, making it as easy as possible for your customers to do business. If unnecessary barriers are placed in the way of the customer journey, then customers may well vote with their feet, particularly when the going gets tough through a pandemic, for example.

Dealing with stakeholders

We all have interested parties in our business life; this could be our family, investors, non-executive directors (NEDs), regulators or government policy makers. The important issue to note here is that we need to keep an eye on the outer factors that influence our inner business circle, such as the board, teams and customers.

We will cover work–life balance at length in the next chapter, but if we ensure that we engage stakeholders in a positive and constructive manner then we will stand a good chance of developing a fully functional and positive culture and working climate that enables all stakeholders to understand and get behind the business mission, which can only mean good working conditions.

That said, we need to welcome challenge from our stakeholders. This is where boards play an important part. If we are to build businesses that disrupt the status quo for the better and build innovative and creative solutions for our markets, then to do so constructively we need challenge. A diversified board or team can engage in taking a vertical and horizontal review of business matters (a tad more holistic than the much-quoted 'root and branch review') and so challenge existing practices that act as inhibitors to growth or the drivers for a constructive culture.

We again need the EQ to understand stakeholders' positions and views and ensure that communications are clear and everyone is on the same page, particularly where strategic decisions are made.

Where it can all go wrong generally is down to one thing: yes, you guessed it, behavioural bias. If we do not employ the right operational and system controls to drive a positive culture, then a number of issues may rear their ugly heads, such as:

- A dysfunctional board

- A domineering CEO

- Posts held by individuals lacking technical competence

- Inadequate four-eyes oversight of risk

- A poor understanding of aggregation of risk

To stop such dysfunctional behaviour in its tracks we can ensure stakeholders are in place to act as a four-eyes sense check, and challenge through asking questions, which might include:

- What proactive steps does the business take to identify the behavioural risks inherent within it?

- How do you encourage individuals to be responsible for managing the conduct and behaviour in their business?

- What support does the firm put in place to enable those who work there to improve their conduct relating to the business function(s)?

- How does the board gain oversight of the conduct of business within their organisation and consider the conduct implications of the strategic decision that they make?

- Has the firm assessed whether there are any other activities it undertakes that could undermine strategies put in place to improve conduct, such as remuneration strategy or complaints handling?

We discount our stakeholders at our peril. Some firms I have worked with do not know who all their stakeholders are. This can be fatal, so ensure you carry out a simple exercise to create a culture for engagement and that all stakeholders are identified, acknowledged and engaged.

Many firms work smart and engage in partnerships or joint ventures which can help leverage business services and products and get them to market fast. An example could be a financial advice firm engaging an accountancy or solicitor firm to offer tax and legal services to their client base. This is of particular importance when we look at the so-called great wealth transfer: the movement of money down the generations, which means Generation X and millennials may well inherit the wealth of baby boomers (born 1946–64) – currently estimated at some £4 trillion.[45]

To encourage the children of their clients to stick with their business, financial advisers are changing their business models and with it their culture. They are becoming financial planners and offering a more holistic coaching and guidance service which leverages external partnerships with portfolio management firms, lawyers and accountants. This is so they can not only offer advice, guidance, long-term care, and will and trust planning aimed at building trust with their existing clients and considering their needs in retirement, but also technology such as apps and cash flow tools that can engage the next generation. In essence, it is those retail investment advice firms who are now offering a family-office-style approach, once the preserve of the ultra-rich, to regular clients. This creates a culture for nurturing client long-term needs and thus a service not a product sell.

One of the best and probably well-known examples of technology firm partnerships was the 1997 deal made between America's two largest computer companies. With one deciding that the business needed a major financial investment to steady the cash flows, they approached their competitor and offered to make their platform along with their browser available for its users as the default in turn for a multimillion-dollar investment and settling all outstanding litigation. They realised that the culture for innovation came before trying to beat their closest rival.

Where it can go horribly wrong

You now have a cultural blueprint for ensuring your business is highly tuned to your clients and stakeholders. By focusing on building relationship capital with all stakeholders and clients, segmenting service and / or product distribution by customer behaviour, and applying EQ with empathy at the heart of all interactions in the customer journey, you will have the best chance of ensuring high engagement, trusting customers and an excellent reputation.

You also need to be aware of biases and how they can undermine all the good work you have done in building loyal stakeholder relationships. This can manifest in many ways:

- Prioritising company policy over customer needs

- Mismanaging social media

- Keeping customers on hold

- Incompetent support

- Comprising customers' personal privacy

Prioritising company policy over customer needs

As we have seen, the NRE demands an agile business that can respond to customers' ever-changing personal needs and requirements. There are plenty of examples where firms do everything by the book on policy and lose customers along the way. This can be due to price-match strategy, which has been shown to provide a false sense of security. Many providers do not actually offer the lowest price, despite their price-matching policy, or they may not apply this to online products, thus creating disparity and mistrust among customers. Of course this can then lead to reputational issues, given the power of social media.

Mismanaging social media

When you send a message or publish a post on social media, you are broadcasting and thus open to potential prosecution if any content may be viewed as libellous, for example. The fact that social media is ever evolving and has such a large reach means the case for engaging the seven strategies in the previous chapter is ever pressing. The dichotomy here is that social media is powerful in instant, real-time information, but a company policy that dictates a four-eyes sense check that can take hours, if not days or weeks, just is not going to cut it. This can lead to a culture of poor customer engagement and insincere responses. Of course, you need to balance any data security and compliance requirements with messaging, but having a constructive social media engagement strategy is now essential to attain responsive and clear communications.

Keeping customers on hold

This is a cardinal sin. You just should not go there. I never forget listening to pop legend and business entrepreneur Bob Geldolf speaking at a conference on trust, in which he stipulated that if a company places you through an automated telephone system and keeps you on hold for any time at all, then they just do not care (his words were more explicit). It's true: you simply cannot keep your customers on hold, whether it's through the telephone, online or face-to-face. Remember that the NRE demands instant data and information; if the next generation are kept on hold, they will simply get bored and move on.

Incompetent support

Relating to the above point, if you have a system that (for example) offers online chat, this can be great if it is aligned to your customer needs and journey, but if your customers get stuck in loops and there is a poor handover to live chat with a customer rep, then there is only one outcome: a frustrated customer. This can easily be avoided by state-of-the-art live chat technology, road mapping customer journeys, and smooth transitions to human support.

Compromising customers' personal privacy

In the EU and UK we all should know the General Data Protection Regulation, where data protection and privacy has been significantly increased from the Data Protection Act. Time after time we see human error still getting in the way, whether it's clicking on that phishing email or losing a memory stick at Heathrow with the Queen's security information, or poor data protection systems leading to the personal data of thousands of customers being breached.

CASE STUDY: Digital networking platform – Octo members

Octo is an extremely dynamic digital community of almost 4,000 individuals, which accepts members from across the financial services ecosystem. We strive to showcase great practitioners, and forward-thinking ideas and products to assist in the delivery of great outcomes to clients. While forums and networking groups have existed for some time, they tend to be based around similar roles, such as financial planners.

Octo is deliberately not part of this. By learning and sharing ideas across financial services, we aim to avoid echo chambers and groupthink.

Great ideas from fintech, regtech, marketing, brand, investment management, practice and personal development and beyond are all fed in alongside financial planning and wealth management content.

Subject matter experts and provider companies in supporting disciplines share their knowledge with those who advise private clients and, in turn, these same advisers share their clients' needs and knowledge with the providers, creating a more informed sector attuned to the needs of the adviser and client.

Our continual programme of debate, articles, interviews and panel sessions, live and on-demand, are supplemented by in-person events.

All of this content distribution is achieved using a highly customised platform, which is licensed from Mighty Networks in the US, with a plug-in for dynamic MI and reporting. As a supported model our MI is key, hence going for a best-in-class reporting system.

Chapter checkpoints

- You should apply technology to your stakeholder engagement strategies. Not doing so could have a significant detrimental effect on your reputation.

- Investigate the value of client surveys. They are worth doing, particularly if you survey the right things, such as how easy it is for clients to do business with you.

- Focus on segmenting clients (not segregating). This will ensure you have the best chance of offering appropriate and suitable products and services and technology to match their ongoing needs.

SEVEN
Your People

In business, the most important piece of the success jigsaw is often considered to be your clients. Well yes and no. Having the right team with a diversified balance of skills across the business structure and roles is crucial to creating the right culture and to the ultimate success of the business enterprise.

We have looked at the rudimentary elements that build culture and seen that it is those organisations that employ the right people – who fit in and grow with the business's long-term vision and short-term mission – that can build the most effective constructive culture. That said, you also need the five keys in place and synced to ensure you are aligned with the NRE.

In Chapter Three I made the case for EQ and organisations showing empathy to their customers and stakeholders. This also means that, in gaining the right culture for growth and responsible business, we need to ensure our staff are big on EQ by introducing a recruitment and staff training and development programme that nurtures and encourages empathy and high relationship capital across departments and relevant teams.

Teams and technology

What is clear when we see constructive culture in action is that it is the people who work in a functional and cohesive manner who create a highly trusting, productive, effective and efficient working environment. To achieve this, the company vision and mission will be integral for setting the tone. A team that is aligned and working towards the same objectives and goals is paramount. We ensure an EQ-driven team by considering the following areas.

Demonstrate strong leadership

In academia there are many theories that focus on effective leadership styles, such as transformational, transactional, leader–member exchange, followership, explicit and implicit. Without getting bogged down in theory, suffice it to say there is no single effective leadership style, but what seems to be constant is the need for leaders to show deep empathy and stay close to and in tune with their team's needs. This means that blending the business vision with everyday team development issues, and demonstrating excellent social skills, or delegating to someone who can act as a 'ringleader', is essential. Teams then feel heard and listened to, there is a willingness to change, excuses are avoided, a helping hand is offered, and the door is kept open. Remember, a good leader who can build a successful, resilient and sustainable team has positive EQ traits: they are self-aware and socially aware, they evoke good emotional management, communicate effectively and excel in conflict resolution.

Identify and accept the strengths and weaknesses of team members

Recognising that team members are people is a good start. Employers and stakeholders have a vast array of talent, skills and knowledge, and harnessing them is crucial to your business success. It is also imperative to understand your team's weaknesses. This is where diagnostic tools such as psychometrics will help. If they are researched well and they have high validity, they can offer data and MI on areas of behaviour or competence you may be unaware of, and thus allow you to design tools and techniques to improve skills and identify roles best suited to certain individuals.

Encourage creativity and innovation

This is essential, particularly if you are a start-up or an SME or you employ a diverse and virtual team of developers. Create time in the diary to have 'creativity hang-outs' where staff are encouraged to speak openly and freely about particular initiatives or projects in play, and encourage a solution-based approach where problems are challenged and solutions suggested. As we know, empathy plays a huge role in creating a constructive culture within your business, and helps business owners understand what motivates their team and the challenges and opportunities they may be experiencing.

Encourage work, rest and play

People need to enjoy 'downtime' and rest to enable creativity and productivity. In his book *The Organized Mind*,[46] Daniel Levitin says, 'Studies have found that productivity goes up when the number of hours per week of work goes down, strongly suggesting that adequate leisure and refuelling time pays off for employers and for workers… a sixty-hour workweek, although 50% longer than a forty-hour workweek, reduces productivity by 25%, so it takes two hours of overtime to accomplish one hour of work.'

Prioritise sleep

According to sleep science, sleep reduces stress and helps people refuel. This can be climate-driven: those people in warmer climates, for example continental Europe, take siestas, which tends to make people happier and means their performance levels also rise, according to *Imagine: How creativity works* by Jonah Lehrer.[47] The National Sleep Foundation states that: 'Naps can restore alertness, enhance performance and reduce mistakes and accidents. A study at NASA on sleepy pilots and astronauts found that a forty-minute nap improved performance by 34% and alertness by 100%.'[48] Some of the most famous nappers in history are Winston Churchill and Albert Einstein, so if you want to prioritise your staff's wellbeing and creativity, encourage short naps or downtime in their working day.

Challenge the status quo

This is essential in avoiding groupthink and a 'yes culture' to appease the senior staff's views and needs, which can derail any organisation large and small. The C-suite should not avoid or quash challenge from their colleagues; indeed they should welcome it, but it should be encouraged in a structured environment – whether that's through meetings, 'challenge sessions' or technology – to promote conflict resolution and provide workable solutions.

Employ enterprise social networking (ESN) technology

This should not be confused with social media, social enterprise (corporate social responsibility (CSR) – more of that later) or social networks like LinkedIn. ESN is a platform on which your workplace communicates.

In the 1990s and 2000s we had intranets that allowed employees to communicate and receive corporate information. With the advancement of AI and machine learning, we now have platforms that encourage social engagement on specific work-related issues and can identify a staff member's skill sets based on how they are communicating on the platform. They can then be deployed more effectively in areas that best suit their skills. ESN technology allows multiple teams and employees to interact all in one place. Many ESNs also offer company-wide announcements and news streams to broadcast company communications and encourage employee advocacy.

Behaviour and groups

What about real life and businesses who inspire their staff to work in teams to reach great heights and achieve great things?

There is evidence that it is those organisations that split their teams into smaller units that gain the best results. It's a bit like a dinner party: you can ask someone on the same table for the salt or pepper, you do not have to delegate or place a special request through a formal system to get stuff done.

It may be helpful to bring in the army here, as armed forces are highly successful in training their soldiers to act on instruction and as a team to achieve specific goals. There is no room for error when they go to war and they tend to work effectively and efficiently to achieve their aims. The army is probably one of the best human resource experiments for us to focus on.

Platoons the size of five have been shown to be highly effective in missions due to their clear communications, team ethic, agreed roles and commitment to acting as a tight unit to achieve the mission in the best possible way. One of the tactics used by Steve Jobs was to break his developers into smaller units and set them each the same task. With smaller teams came more agility and innovation and, upon gaining the results, Jobs could then ascertain which teams were on track, take key learnings from the outcome and reload the teams to go again, refining the process until he got what he wanted.

Using smaller teams is a great way to break down risk and gain a better view on risk management. For example, in *Noise*[49] Kahneman et al found that breaking a business project into manageable steps and allocating them to individual teams can assist risk-based decision-making by ensuring a diversified approach towards each segment. These can then be pooled, and the better ideas used across the whole risk-management process. This means using 'broad framing' – seeing a decision as one of a class of decisions, rather than one big decision.

NINE TIPS TO BUILD A GREAT TEAM

1. Set specific goals for the team
2. Onboard new team members carefully

3. Nip toxic behaviour in the bud
4. Don't be afraid of different viewpoints
5. Set aside time
6. Address the past and move on
7. Look beyond your own bias
8. Deal with process, not content
9. Design and agree a value statement

Organisational structure, leadership and followership

As we discussed in Chapter Five, the NRE and personalisation have dramatically changed the way we do business. Clients need to experience the product or service you are selling them, they need to know it makes their personal and/or working life easier, and they want turnkey solutions with high value. This means the old-style hierarchical organisational structures are no longer fit for purpose. Businesses are now operating what I call a 'flat' structure where all staff activities and skill sets are valued equally and communication lines are streamlined so vital market information, risk or client, can be communicated quickly to the key business decision-making channels.

This also means the business structure needs to embrace transformation and be open to change. As we have seen, in their book *Beyond Great* Bhattacharya, Lang and Hemerling argue it is those businesses who can organise in a focused, fast and flat way that can respond to the new demands of twenty-first-century business.[50] This is important, as business models that rely on traditional, slow, paper-based decision-making processes will miss big opportunities. Customised communication channels across a flat organisational structure mean stakeholders will be aligned and the organisation will demonstrate resilient and evidence-based decision-making – something that a black swan event like a pandemic demands.

Of course, those organisations who wish to offer high value for all stakeholders need to nurture both leadership and followership. Too many publications on leadership tend to focus on a top-down approach – ie using leadership styles, tools and techniques as a way of encouraging others to take the desired action. The importance of followership has been understated over the years.

Scholars of business strategy will be familiar with the leadership styles and their characteristics in the table below.

Leadership styles

Style	Characteristics
Transactional	Work and reward
Transformational	Inspirational
Situational	Adaptable
Laissez-faire	Hands-off
Participative	Collaborative

It is up to you which leadership style(s) you wish to develop, but you need to keep in mind your team's and clients' needs and, in particular, how follower-ship relates to leadership styles.

Any high-performing sports team will tell you that there are leaders throughout the team. In any hierar-chical structure, including business culture, followers are just as important as leaders. The old adage that 'without his armies, Napoleon was just a man with grandiose ambitions' means that, although leaders matter greatly, organisations stand or fall partly on the basis of how well their leaders lead and how well their followers follow.

There is now a whole raft of social science around followership and how it can redefine business suc-cess. According to Robert Kelley,[51] the four steps that can develop good followers are:

1. Redefine followership and leadership roles as equal but different activities

2. Teach skills that make effective followers

3. Evaluate performance of followership capacities

4. Build structures such as leaderless groups and rotate leadership assignments

Examples abound on how strong teamwork can benefit from a strong followership. A classic exam-ple is that of the culture carriers: people who take accountability and responsibility for facilitating and embedding constructive culture across the business. Hewlett-Packard developed their 'HP way' by reflect-ing their values in everyday life at the company: trust and respect, high achievement, integrity, teamwork, flexibility and innovation.

Followership is important because firms need to walk their talk so that a good culture permeates through their operations, systems, controls, teams, services and products. It is also a way to ensure that egos are kept in check: placing others, the team, first is crucial in establishing a constructive culture.

Culture carriers

Encouraging employees and teams to become culture carriers is essential, and followership can help. It empowers individuals to think critically about business decisions, and to see strategy, such as client-centricity and teamwork, as a collective or silo orientation. In their book *Built to Last*, Jim Collins and Jerry Porras describe the intensely potent culture of Nordstrom.[52] Individuals who fit Nordstrom's culture are happy and fulfilled, and they do not leave.

Being a culture carrier means strong followership and leadership traits are required to ensure emotional engagement, intelligence and commitment throughout the business. Good culture carriers are infectious and spread company values quickly and effectively. It is essential the corporate leadership think carefully about the business values, and a good place to start would be with its people.

In my business, our values are based on not taking our eyes off the PRIZE:

- Positivity means embracing challenges, communicating potential and learning from perceived failures.

- Resilience involves patience and persistence, learning when and when not to push, and building our team reserves to keep going when times get tough.

- Integrity means being authentic and honest at all times, speaking our truth and respecting others.

- Zing is all about focus, energy and optimisation – think Tigger from *Winnie the Pooh*. Building a business is hard work: we need to make sure our team have the right energy to create, innovate and implement but also have time to reflect and recharge.

- Empathy is playing back to EQ, placing ourselves in each other shoes, understanding and respecting other viewpoints, and coming to informed decisions that incorporate stakeholders' views.

Cultural change

Change is a natural part of life, yet it tends to be feared, particularly in business strategy and management. The key to change is people and their behaviour. If a leader wants to change direction and encourage a culture change then it is not just new policies, processes and systems that will achieve this. To achieve collective change over time, mentoring, role modelling and applying diagnostic profile assessments, learning and development programmes are all necessary to encourage people to buy in and go with the new change journey rather than defend the status quo.

When it comes to mentorship and role modelling, this means leaders need to walk their talk and act out the new cultural drivers they want to attain. The fundamental problem with cultural change is people and their inability to align their internal values with those they are reflecting externally. Think about it: the most sustainably successful leaders and their organisations are perfectly synced when putting their words into action. They inspire staff, use metrics such as behavioural science (identifying and managing biases), intuitive psychometrics – personality tests – and good old learning and development programmes to transfer learning to everyday activities and tasks.

Mentorship and role modelling

Starting with leadership or followership, the 'influencers' should be completely and wholeheartedly committed to change that is conducted with an ethical and people-focused approach. Mentorship helps individuals connect their deeper human motivations and values to their careers, and aligning these two will pay dividends to employers and employees alike. According to Gallup, nearly 85% of employees worldwide are still not engaged or are actively disengaged at work, despite greater effort from companies.[53]

Loneliness is a concurrent pandemic, with 65% of young people in a recent University of Miami study reporting increased loneliness since the start of the Covid-19 pandemic, and 80% reporting 'significant depressive symptoms'.[54] The UK government is currently grappling with the fact that over 500,000 have left the workforce since the pandemic started.

When it comes to role modelling, clarity of purpose, creating benchmarks, celebrating wins, checking in, mapping progress and encouraging engagement are just some of the key strategies that must be actioned and seen by staff if confidence and trust are to be gained and maintained in the change programme.

Behavioural science, people and change

Cultural change means behavioural change, so we ideally need to understand the decision-making processes of our leaders and staff, and this includes bias management. Some of the most successful strategies I have witnessed in my career are simple:

- **Positive messaging that reflects the company's core values:** Whether it's on an intranet, social enterprise platform or inside the walls of the office, making consistent messaging available at all times to staff will ensure the message sticks.

- **Personal development planning and journaling:** The power of writing down goals and objectives, and overcoming challenges and strategy, can motivate the subconscious brain to find solutions and bring them into the conscious world through action.

- **Endowment effect:** As we have seen, this is all about emotional attachment causing an individual to value an owned object higher (often irrationally) than its market value: one of the best biases if ever there was one.

- **Gamification:** Remember, good technology is an enabler. Involving staff in their goal planning and allowing them 'skin in the game' means they tend to buy in at a deeper level. This can be through a variety of ways, not just economic incentives.

- **Social norms:** Finding what motivates the individual is powerful; some may find increased holiday allocation and / or flexible working far more valuable than economic incentives.

- **Scoring norms:** Points and rewards can be used to enthuse performance and a variety of benefits can be provided, such as a trip to a countryside retreat.

- **Risk management:** Using technology to support decision-making is central to my culture coding message. Inadequate risk management is at the heart of any dysfunctional culture, so whether it is staff training and development, stakeholder or client engagement (see the case study at the end of the chapter), using technology to identify, monitor and manage risk is essential.

Depending on if and how the business is regulated, these strategies can forge strong bonds with staff and allow them to pursue their career goals within the organisation rather than stick around in a traditionally economy-driven environment, which can lead to shallow buy-in and a willingness to move for similar economic means.

Your people and resilience

As you may well have noticed, resilience is a common theme throughout this book. We're coming out of the tail end of a pandemic and the resilience shown by society and business to get through this unprecedented event has been impressive.

Despite furlough, personal and economic difficulties, there are many stories of people taking a positive view and embracing new challenges in business. Whether that's learning new skills, a language or musical instrument, or spending more time in nature, people have shown they are adaptable and can survive.

It is this adaptability that companies need to harness to come out the other side of the pandemic stronger (no, I'm not going down the route of the government mantra of 'Bounce Back Better'). For example, they may learn that remote working makes some staff more productive and happier, as they're around for their family, and use technology to adapt and action their activities online.

When it comes to culture coding, it's all about understanding your people: understanding what motivates them, getting under the bonnet of their thinking and tailoring work ergonomics to fit the worker (not the other way around). The goal should be to eliminate physical and emotional discomfort at work.

Wellbeing in the workplace

In any discussion of key HRD strategies, such as recruitment, retention and engagement, it's worth revisiting another issue you need to factor in – wellbeing.

Measuring wellbeing is crucial to assessing individual motivations and ensuring you have the right people not just for production but also the welfare of your staff – they are both interrelated and cannot be separated. To define wellbeing in the workplace, a good place to start is with 'affect'. This is an umbrella term encompassing a broad range of moods and emotions that individuals experience, which means it is important to understand and apply EQ and its five attributes.

Emotional regulation (influence), contagion (transfer) and labour (suppression) are key issues that, if left unaddressed, can spill over into producing anxiety and stress within the workforce, leading to a potentially unsuccessful cultural outcome.

The below diagram can help define affect within organisations, and plot structures, systems, controls, policies and procedures that produce a negative and positive affect.[55] The ideal is to create a blend of the right side of the circumplex by using trial and error to map out strategies that work and eliminate those that do not.

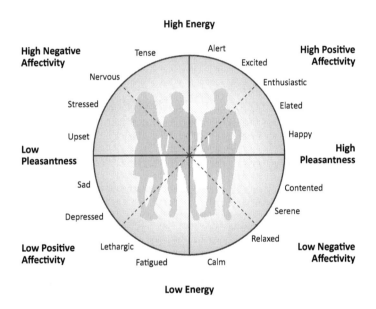

The circumplex model of affect: 'The affective circumplex'
(adapted from L Feldman Barrett and J Russell, 1998[56])

Collaborative challenge and creativity at work

This is an interesting concept if you want your organisation to foster a creative culture. Organisations are 'affectively' laden environments – you only have to look at creative individuals such as John Lennon and

Paul McCartney from The Beatles, technology 'gurus' such as PayPal co-founders Peter Thiel and Elon Musk: they were at their most creative when in an environment of 'collaborative challenge'. If you can harness high positive and a small amount of high negative affectivity, then this could drive creative activity.

Motivation and performance

When it comes to social science, my favourite theory in relation to motivation is the wonderfully named Vroom's expectancy theory, which separates effort, performance and outcomes.[57] Vroom assumes that behaviour results from conscious choices whose purpose is to maximise pleasure and minimise pain.

Vroom realised that an employee's performance is based on individual factors such as personality, skills, knowledge, experience and abilities. He states that effort, performance and motivation are linked in a person's motivation. This is based in three variables: expectancy (increased effort will increase performance), instrumentality (good performance means outcomes are achieved) and valence (perceived value the employee puts on the outcome). This means, from a cultural perspective, we need to have the right people in the right place with the right skills, along with the right motivational frameworks.

When it comes to performance, you can't beat Mihaly Csikszentmihalyi's flow theory.[58] Csikszent-mihalyi is considered one of the founders of positive psychology and was the first to identify and research 'flow states'. In interviewing athletes, musicians and artists, Csikszentmihalyi found that their optimal performance was when they were in a flow state; in other words, their work simply appeared to flow out of them without much effort.

Think of a time when you have been in a state of mind where you're happy and in the zone, everything you are doing seems easy and you're gaining great results. That's flow state. In terms of culture coding, you have to remove any external (systems, controls) or internal (biases, negative emotions) barriers that may get in the way of such states of high motivation and performance. You need to be mindful when recruiting staff that you have the right environment to empower flow states.

This may sound relatively easy, but it isn't. You only have to ask any performer in sports, the arts or business; they generally cannot tell you how they managed to attain or sustain flow state. Malcolm Gladwell explained the 10,000-hours rule in his book *Outliers,* stipulating that it takes 10,000 hours of intensive practice to master complex skills and materials.[59] It is hard to argue against this, particularly if you look at examples such as The Beatles' Hamburg and Cavern days pre Beatlemania, or Bill Gates's programming work before founding his technology empire; yet surely it is also about the quality of practice along with the quantity?

The below diagram shows Csikszentmihalyi's flow model in action. As Csikszentmihalyi stated, flow is 'a state in which people are so involved in an activity that nothing else seems to matter; the experience is so enjoyable that people will continue to do it even at great cost, for the sheer sake of doing it.'[60] Sounds addictive, right? As the diagram illustrates, those who put the work in, increase their skill sets and set them to meet high challenges can gain flow state. If you ask anyone who has attained this, they will probably tell you they had no idea how they got there and achieved the great things they achieved in that state – it just happens.

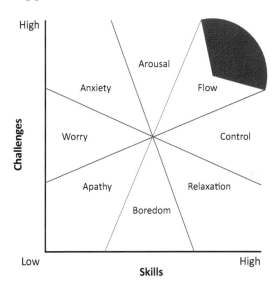

Csikszentmihalyi's flow model
(adapted from Csikszentmihalyi, 1990[61])

To gain flow you can take some straightforward actions, which include:

- Set specific work goals that stretch abilities. Setting stretch goals can be tricky because you need to take great care in setting them at the right level – ie not too low (apathy, boredom, relaxation) or too high (worry, anxiety). Tailoring goals and making them realistic is key, and there are various ways to do this. You may have heard of specific, measurable, accurate, realistic, time-bound, ecological and reviewed (SMARTER) goal setting, for example.

- Schedule and protect 'deep work' time. Professor Cal Newport developed the deep work concept,[62] which involves commitment and consistency to get the most out of flow. Professor Newport stipulated it only takes three to four hours of undisturbed, continuous deep work to see transformational change in productivity.

- Take short breaks. Studies have shown the brain tends to need a break after sixty to ninety minutes of concentration. They also show that productivity can increase if rest time is incorporated into the working day.

- Maintain a flow-friendly workplace and use technology to measure flow states.

- Apply the right technology to encourage motivation (eg gamification) and collaboration across areas such as e-learning, client engagement and everyday activities, but remember to assure employees that technology is an enabler not a replacement.

Applying these practices can help develop what Csik-szentmihalyi calls an 'autotelic personality', which describes a person who 'is never bored, seldom anxious, involved with what goes on and in flow most of the time'.[63]

Recruitment, training and reward recognition

Your staff embody the culture you are trying to build, so, along with ensuring the framework is designed constructively, it is imperative that you recruit, train and retain the right people. Individual attributes such as resilience, accountability, achievement orientation, affiliation, selflessness, teamwork, adaptability, efficiency and effectiveness are all desirable behaviours.

Without engaged employees, followers who also inspire leadership and vice versa, your business will be lost. You need to ensure you have a recruitment proposition that is geared to attracting the right people who will fit in with and enhance the desired culture.

Where business performance fails, this can generally be down to mismanaged bias and behaviours, and dysfunctional decision-making. 'A bold statement,' I hear you say. Well yes, but the premise of this book is that constructive culture coding can only be attained if we ensure we have the right preferences, beliefs, habits, behaviours and values in place. This starts and ends with our people and that includes those at the top.

Where we see this going wrong is generally down to the failure of a firm's internal controls and inadequate governance. As we have seen, a firm that can gain buy-in to their mission and vision statements, code of conduct or values stands a better chance of building the constructive culture they need to thrive in a relationship-driven economy.

There is no better man to explain how we incentivise our people and manage their biases than Daniel Ariely, who is responsible for waking me up to the need for business to identify and manage biases to ensure functional decision-making across risk, operational and service management.

In his book *The Honest Truth About Dishonesty*, Ariely points to the 'fudge factor' that can cause mayhem in the workplace.[64] The fudge factor theory states that humans desire to secure the benefits of cheating but simultaneously view ourselves as honest people. This bias is known as cognitive dissonance, in that we can hold two conflicting beliefs, values or moral principles at the same time.

Moral licensing has a big part to play in compliance and ethics in business and establishing a culture that promotes an ethical environment. When people decide to comply or not, they review whether they have been absolved of the need to hold themselves to certain standards and thus gain a belief or moral licence to pursue their self-interest. An example of this is financial advice and bias. Financial advisers need to disclose any conflicts of interest, yet behavioural science tells us that once any are disclosed, the more unscrupulous advisers may see the right to deliver biased advice.

Understanding why people cheat can be a good benchmark for having the right control mechanisms in place to recruit, train and incentivise staff in the right ways. Ariely found that people would cheat 'a little bit' to enable them to gain desired results and justify this against their own moral coding or standards.

Biases that are left unmanaged, such as overconfidence, loss aversion, the endowment effect, groupthink and cognitive dissonance, can lead to a highly dysfunctional culture, dishonesty and organisational failure. You only have to look at what happened to Royal Bank of Scotland in the financial crises in 2008–2009 to see these biases and more in action.

Diversity and inclusion

From experience, when it comes to professions such as the financial service industry, there is still too much influence from male-dominated boards made up of people with degrees from elite universities, yet times are changing. A recent report by the Financial Reporting Council (FRC) on board diversity and effectiveness in FTSE 350 companies shows a 36% increase in women on FTSE boards.[65] It highlights the hallmarks of boards with more women included as:

- Significantly greater decentralisation in operations

- Increased likelihood of reaching consensus

- Reduced overconfidence about the board's problem-solving skills

Ethnicity is also an issue, with the FRC citing only 7% of boards have directors from ethnic minorities. We are now seeing a regulatory push, with the diversity and inclusion (D&I) rules of the UK financial services regulator, the Financial Conduct Authority (FCA), requiring that listed companies have a minimum of 40% of women on their board, with at least one senior board member being a woman and at least one member being from an ethnic minority background.[66] The FRC report shows that those firms with at least one woman on their board have a three to five percentage points higher EBITDA (earnings before interest, taxes, depreciation and amortisation) margin. Case closed.

Given the NRE, I would also argue that boards need to ensure they have at least one individual with digital skills and strong technology understanding; otherwise they will quickly be left behind when meeting client, business and market needs.

CASE STUDY: Aveni

Aveni is an award-winning fintech based in Edinburgh in the UK. The firm uses generative AI and natural language processing (NLP) to automate business processes, and actionable insights in financial service firms using the voice of the customer. The business comprises a unique combination of financial services professionals with deep technology expertise and works with leading blue-chip financial services firms.

Over the last couple of years, there have been major advances in machine learning and NLP that have enabled automated analytics to monitor every customer interaction. More recently, LLMs have captured the public's imagination and will fundamentally transform the way businesses operate.

Aveni is working at the leading edge of technology, which it believes is becoming increasingly central to the operating models of financial services firms. Those at the forefront of adaptation are already benefitting from greater productivity, oversight, business and people performance and revenue growth. This gulf will increase over time.

Chapter checkpoints

- Focus on a creative culture and employ ESN technology and algorithms to enable your people to thrive and grow with your business, sharing ideas and information and making informed choices.

- Understand how your culture encourages work and wellbeing and motivates your staff positively.

- Lead but do not discount the concept of followership. Identify your culture carriers and avoid complacency that can breed dysfunctional culture and negative bias.

- Employ D&I and ensure you have at least one technology-savvy board or senior team member.

- Bring your staff along with you on the technology and AI journey by engaging technology specialists and creating clear communications and tailored technology training and development programmes.

EIGHT

Your Systems

We now live in a world where most of the gadgets in Star Trek's original series from the 1960s are with us: computers that talk and provide real-time information and advice (think Alexa or Siri), tablet computers and smartphones enabling instant communications, universal translators and much more.

The pace of digital change is so fast. New opportunities and challenges are emerging every day and the next decade will see huge advancements, particularly in the world of AI and machine learning, with the internet and e-commerce offering infinite possibilities for business to operate with ease in the global economy.

Just think about it: anyone can set up a business in their own home and gain instant brand recognition by creating a social media account, a social media group or a video channel on streaming platforms, all for free.

The root to success is still not a given even in the digital economy; what is needed are the right strategies, people, policies, systems and controls, and digital systems to build a constructive culture that can take advantage of this digital revolution.

The digital revolution and the new relationship economy

The NRE – which demands subscription models, a digital turnkey experience and instant (real-time) information and data to make informed choices – is now an opportunity for businesses to further develop products and services that can enable their customers to gain the experience they desire. This involves several features and benefits.

Technology as a facilitator

Having the right technology across systems, controls, operations and services can enable you to develop and embrace a constructive culture. ESN technology is a good example: this is a private, internal social network you can use to facilitate safe communications within your teams. Think team messaging, project and task management, and collaboration tools on one platform.

ESNs help you fill communication gaps, encourage sales performance and manage ongoing activities. The systems also provide valuable data analytics that can identify an individual's behaviours and skill sets, and whether projects are working well and messages are communicated clearly. They are invaluable in spreading the right activities and messages to encourage the desired culture.

OSS is also central to modern technology in its ability to facilitate business agility and tailor third-party software to a company's ongoing needs, which no doubt will change over time.

Data analytics

Technology embedded correctly within your business will not only enable streamlined front-line services, but it will also help provide data analytics so you can deep dive into evidence for constructive or dysfunctional staff behaviours or system performance that can support or disrupt (sometimes terminally) your best business endeavours.

When it comes to starting and running your business, it is imperative to collect relevant data and MI so you can identify strengths and weaknesses and make better decisions. Data analytics enables key strategic initiatives and improves relationships with clients, customers, business stakeholders and partners.

One of the key components to data is its quality. 'Rubbish in, rubbish out' is the mantra. This is problematic as low-quality data adversely impacts many areas of business performance. It can result in wasted marketing, incomplete client and prospect data, increased spending, and decision-making that is detrimental to the business. It is imperative firms know they are always collecting high-quality and relevant data.

One way to do this is to gather a list of data records, focus on your top ten key data elements and run through each data record to identify noticeable errors. Once you have run through this exercise you should have two tables: one for perfect records and another for records with errors, showing the quality level of your data.

Data and EBP

One of the most important areas where technology and data can add huge value to your business's cultural development is the GRC strategy – that 'business prevention unit' that many firms want to avoid with a passion. If you are engaged via regtech, your conduct and culture can be better assessed through MI and data that provides themes and trends across their cultural growth.

We already know that it is imperative to have a functional and diversified board, a clear decision-making process, accurate systems and controls, and individuals with the right skills and behaviours. Regtech, a type of fintech that allows firms to assess and audit their GRC management against the regulations they must comply with, can ensure your company has all the real-time data and MI you require, presented in an engaging format so you can improve your weaknesses and sustain strengths. Using an approach such as gamification can make GRC an enjoyable exercise, encourage your firm to become more consistent in its approach to audits and gain valuable data that evidences you are standing by your values.

The mantra around compliance used to be: 'If it's not written down it didn't happen.' Well that's gone, and it is now (as previously mentioned): 'If you haven't got the data, it didn't happen.' You could also add: 'If you haven't got the data, it better have happened.'

Other data management tips are:

- Move all your data to a centralised database to create a standardised data architecture.

- Ensure your employees are up to date on all aspects of data best practices, including data entry, management, compliance and safety.

- If you have multiple teams, create data management hierarchies to keep them organised and reduce the odds of a breach occurring.

- Designate certain team members to handle core data management.

It is also important that the right tools are used to ensure high-quality data and access to this data. You can review tools and technologies for accurate data analysis across:

- Data normalisation for simple organisation

- Shareable dashboards for streamlined communication between team members

- Third-party integration

It is also imperative to conduct your own research and due diligence on third-party tools to ensure they are fit for purpose.

AI and machine learning

Everybody seems to be talking about AI, particularly in the context of business strategy. I've seen plenty of start-ups with AI in the company name, even though I see no evidence that AI is being used.

There is currently great anticipation for new LLM machine learning technologies, which are multimodal and will enable further time saving and innovations on report writing and administrative tasks. With Mark Zuckerberg running hard to deliver the 'metaverse', and other big technology companies striving to build robotics such as autonomous vehicles, drones and warehouse robots, it all feels like the new 'gold rush'.

A good place to start to understand all this would be to define AI. The 'father' of computer science, Alan Turing, published a paper in 1950 entitled *Computing Machinery and Intelligence*, which can be viewed as the first time AI was considered, as Turing asked the question, 'Can machines think?'[67] From this point, Turing offered a test (known as the Turing test) where a human interrogator would try to distinguish between a human and computer text response.

We then had Norvig and Russell's *Artificial Intelligence: A modern approach*, which is viewed as a leading AI textbook covering four AI goals in its discussion of systems that act and think like humans and the ideal approach for systems that act and think rationally.[68]

Simply put, AI is a field which combines computer science with robust data sets to enable problem-solving. There are two AI strategies to consider:

1. **Rules-based AI** produces predefined (deterministic) outcomes that are based on a set of rules coded by humans. This system is called simple AI and uses two components: a set of rules and a set of facts.

2. **Machine learning AI** defines its own sets of rules that are based on data outputs. This system is based on a probabilistic approach (generating a catalogue of all possible events); thus machine learning can provide a comprehensive picture for risk management.

There are differences between rules-based AI and machine learning:

- Machine learning models require far more data than rules-based systems. Rules-based systems can operate with a simple data-driven framework.

- Rules-based AI can be designed for specific tasks that need an algorithm to aid decision-making – eg specific compliance and risk-management tasks. Machine learning constantly evolves and adapts in accordance with training using statistical rules, and over time can offer more in-depth and granular MI.

In summary, rules-based systems are immutable (unchanging) whereas machine learning systems are mutable. Rules-based AI will require human intervention to change the algorithms, with training; machine learning can transform over time.

Algorithms and decision-making

In their book *Noise*, Kahneman, Sunstein and Sibony make the case for using behavioural science in decision-making.[69] They provide the reader with plenty of examples of how subconscious bias (skewed thinking) and noise (the variability of errors or inaccurate decision-making) can cause real problems, particularly when it comes to risk management. Two wrongs don't make a right and, when they collude, bias and noise contribute to significant failures in accuracy due to unwanted variability in their decision-making.

For example, the authors describe how doctors tend to prescribe more antibiotics, painkillers or tests in the afternoon than they do in the morning; judges come to different sentences from the same case details and their judgements are affected by the weather. In one example, 208 US federal judges were set the same sixteen cases, which you would expect them to agree on as a whole, but the average difference between the judgement of two judges was three and a half years. This is just based on noise, not bias.

Corporate boards can be male-dominant and led by strong personalities, and the science tells us that those who speak first and have the loudest voice tend to sway opinion. What if they're wrong in their judgement?

Like fish in a tank that can't see the water they swim in, humans don't realise they are surrounded by bias or noise and inaccurate decision-making, which can have devastating effects on everyday activities and business performance. In our world, GRC with regulations means we need to be aware of the muddy water such bias and noise can cause.

'What is the answer?' I hear you asking. Well, algorithms and simple rules tend to be noise free, as long as they manage the bias element. For the foreseeable future, GRC management has human-driven decision-making, which carries the risk of noise and bias getting in the way. We need simple rules, frameworks and algorithms to help us make more accurate compliance-based decisions.

This doesn't mean supplanting judgement with algorithms, but using a cyber approach with AI and human decision-making can make for more accurate outcomes and sound risk management. For instance, regtech can offer AI text analysis to run client file reviews across auto-auditing compliance policy documents, helping auditors signpost strengths and weaknesses, or provide heat-mapped compliance dashboards and push alerts to highlight areas for action.

Personality assessment can also help. As we have seen, emotional intelligence is a prized skill in corporate decision-making. With social skills comes the need to listen, not listen to speak but listen to understand before replying.

A blend of technology, teamwork, decision rules (algorithms) and being mindful when taking those big decisions can certainly help us when we're applying judgement to everyday compliance issues. As *Noise* illustrates, one of the key tools to manage such cognitive dysfunctions as noise and bias is applying algorithms as a decision sense check. Greg Davies, Head of Behavioural Science at Oxford Risk, shows us how algorithms can be seen as decision prosthetics, enabling humans to make more accurate and bias- and noise-free decisions.

CASE STUDY: Greg Davies, PHD, speaking on decision prosthetics, open banking and APIs

Humans are great, but they make systematic mistakes in every field. From chefs using scales, writers using editors and sports people using coaches to doctors following checklists, even the most skilled technicians use tools to ensure consistency.

Technology is also great. Well-designed digital platforms can deliver information to clients that is automatically personalised, easy to use and shaped by its users' behaviours. Technology can turn outputs of a creative process into algorithms, saving human energy for appreciating the ambiguity inherent in their interpretation.

The combination can lead clients through decisions in a tailored fashion, with the tool learning and refining as it goes, like a limb that isn't just strapped on but wired into neural networks. Investor–investment interactions are as constant as the changes that surround them. If the investor is changing, their prosthetics technology needs to be wired in such a way it not only stays attached but learns and adapts along the way.

In many ways this simply reflects how human advisers' subjective understanding of their clients' needs already deepens over time; but, with advanced data analytics, gamification and, potentially, machine learning, we are coming to the point where we can blur the distinction between formal profiling and the understanding of an adviser's client. This creates a digital profiling process that complements and enhances the essential human side of investing.

Systems that combine human and non-human elements can be greater than the sum of their parts. In complex environments that involve human values, ambiguity and changing rules of the game, the human–machine hybrids tend to win out against the independent human or machine competition. Robust, reliable and repeatable insights are hard to scale. Creating recipes is an art but sticking to them consistently (and enabling others to do so too) is a science. Gut instincts should be trusted, but verified, and guided to where they can be most helpful. It's time to give financial decisions a helping prosthetic hand.

Algorithms and risk management

As we can see from the below figure, there are many reasons for developing and implementing algorithms within your business. Given the topic of this book, the area that interests me most is risk management.

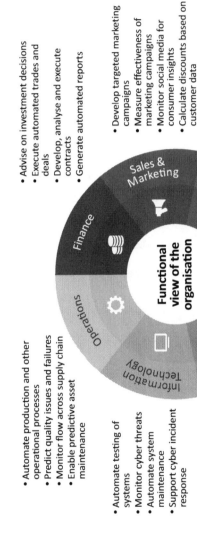

- Advise on investment decisions
- Execute automated trades and deals
- Develop, analyse and execute contracts
- Generate automated reports

- Develop targeted marketing campaigns
- Measure effectiveness of marketing campaigns
- Monitor social media for consumer insights
- Calculate discounts based on customer data

- Effective reporting to the board
- Internal audit activities
- Adequacy and effectiveness of systems and controls
- Evidence-based practice
- Data and management information

- Identify, prioritise and monitor risks
- Spot fraud and conduct investigations
- Analyse business ecosystems
- Enforce regulatory compliance

- Support workforce planning
- Source, recruit and hire talent
- Manage performance of employees
- Increase employee engagement and retention

- Automate testing of systems
- Monitor cyber threats
- Automate system maintenance
- Support cyber incident response

- Automate production and other operational processes
- Predict quality issues and failures
- Monitor flow across supply chain
- Enable predictive asset maintenance

Finance

Sales & Marketing

Governance & Compliance

Risk Management

Human Resources

Information Technology

Operations

Functional view of the organisation

Organisational functions, algorithms and their relationships

What is clear is that whatever form of technology and systems you apply to your business operations and services, it is inevitable that you will be compelled to engage in some form of AI in the not-too-distant future.

In my industry, financial services, we are witnessing an increase in market participants at least thinking about adopting AI and algorithms to make their business more efficient. The FCA and Bank of England published a paper, *Machine Learning in UK Financial Services*, which outlines the perceived benefits in fraud protection, anti-money laundering, operation efficiency and new analytical insights which could lead to new types of product offerings.[70] Machine learning is now at the forefront of cybersecurity.

The risk here is in the need for business to keep pace with machine learning developments. In risk management, it is important the organisation asks practical questions across data security, what metrics should be used to measure its performance, and how many technology and/or AI vendors the business should engage.

Managing the AI downside

Watch out for the naysayers. 'Luddites Destroy Robots' may make an attention-grabbing headline, yet with all the hype around job losses caused by machine learning and AI we need to gain some perspective on where we're at and where we're heading.

Ned Ludd certainly caused a stir in 1779 when he smashed a weaving machine in frustration at his own economic predicament. In the ensuing industrial revolution in the late eighteenth and early nineteenth centuries, labour-saving machinery contributed to job creation and economic demand, and the newly established social science of economics argued that unemployment caused by machinery would be addressed by the upsurge in economic growth.

The first reason to reject the Luddite fallacy is economic theory: companies introduce machines because they increase production and cut costs. This in turn builds economic wealth and demand for labour and creates new jobs.

The second is history: there are more people employed today than since the start of the industrial revolution. If the Luddite fallacy was correct, we'd all be unemployed by now.

What about the current 'digital revolution'? As machine learning offers cognitive skills, will the robots steal jobs that we cannot replace?

One of the most powerful authors on AI and technological unemployment is Martin Ford. In his books *The Lights in the Tunnel* and *Rule of the Robots*, Ford argues AI systems are on the verge of wholesale automation of white-collar jobs – ie jobs involving pattern recognition and information processing.[71]

In their article, 'Four fundamentals of workplace automation', McKinsey consultancy identified 2,000 activities (such as greeting customers, demonstrating products) for a selection of occupations (eg retail sales) that were susceptible to automation.[72] They noted that 5% of jobs were capable of full automation but 60% could have 30% automation if their constituent activities were automated. The report concluded that people will become more productive as machines enable human performance.

This is where AI comes in. If you've ever seen AI play football, you will know the team will not win the World Cup. It is important to note that AI did not rise naturally but was created by humans. Some prefer the term 'machine intelligence', given that cars are not called 'artificial horses' or planes 'artificial birds'.

AI can now help humans with games and puzzles, map searches, self-driving vehicles, and search, image and speech recognition. AI is also in the early days of emotion detection. In retail financial services AI is now helping with:

- Auto-rebalancing and tax harvesting of investment portfolios

- Syncing with your bank account, providing guidance around your savings and spending behaviours

- Providing risk and audit management through regulation technology platforms

- Fighting cybercrime through fraud detection

- Stock traders managing their emotional impulses through biometric technology

- Driving customer-centricity through 'hyperpersonalisation' services – eg identifying customers' spending patterns, financial transactions or travel behaviour

There is also the issue of the machine-executable reporting initiative, where current regulators are looking at how machines can interpret their rules, apply them to organisations in a highly relevant manner and report back accordingly.

AI and bias

If you search the internet for AI robots and select images, you may quickly realise that the vast majority of robot images are white. There is a bias problem in designing algorithms and bot hardware. Examples abound, such as:

- **Racism embedded in US healthcare:** In October 2019 researchers found that an algorithm used on more than 200 million people in US hospitals to predict which patients needed more care heavily favoured white over black patients. It has also been reported that algorithms rejected a disproportionate number of pictures of women with darker skin when measuring them against UK passport rules.

- **Recruitment algorithms:** In 2015 a leading online shopping platform realised that their automated hiring system was biased against women, as the algorithm was based on the number of CVs submitted over the last decade. Since most of the applicants were men, it was trained in favour of men.

- **Algorithms predicting criminal offending:** In May 2016 it was reported an online crime prevention platform was racially biased, with analysts finding the system predicted that black defendants pose a higher risk of reoffending than white defendants.

In her book *Weapons of Math Destruction,* Cathy O'Neil analyses how the use of big data and algorithms in a variety of fields can lead to poor decisions that harm the poor, reinforce racism and amplify inequality.[73]

O'Neil argues, for example, that if a student from a low-income background cannot get a loan due to a lending model deeming her too risky (by virtue of a postcode), she's then cut off from the kind of education that could pull her out of poverty. O'Neil suggests these problematic tools share three key features:

1. Opaque

2. Unregulated

3. Difficult to contest and scalable

Our EQ model shows us that careful research and due diligence are required if we are to employ algorithms built by third parties, and we also need to ensure we have a bias management approach and algorithms designed objectively for the tasks in hand.

We are now at the start of a new age where machines will genuinely self-learn and provide efficiency which will in turn provide cost and time savings; however, people buy people, and there are two key issues to consider here:

1. While AI cannot match human capability, there is a need for a cyber approach where humans can blend machine with personal services.

2. As we have seen with the Luddite fallacy, new technology creates a new space, new opportunities and new economic opportunities.

As I keep telling my two children, many jobs they can apply for when they reach the age for joining the workforce are yet to be created. With the rise of machine learning, there will be new opportunities that require the humanities, soft skills and emotional intelligence that AI will always be challenged to replace.

The future's bright for humans; we just need to keep doing what we're best at: adapting to working with AI-driven machines.

Changing the way you make decisions

As you may well guess, I argue strongly that the premise to gaining a constructive culture code within your business is to place technology right at the centre of all you do. We know technology is not magic, but with careful research, due diligence and strategic planning, you can apply the right technologies within the systems and controls for all your activities to ensure you are fit for purpose in the NRE.

This means you can quickly identify, manage and eradicate dysfunctional behaviours caused by biases. Moral coding is something which is now on the agenda for most industries when it comes to gaining the right employees, clients and customer engagement. As we have seen, EQ is the new benchmark for employee performance and customer retention so you can be confident you have staff with the right attitudes who blend well with your governance and compliance requirements.

The table below illustrates the need to take what I call a 'cyber strategy'. This means using a blend of technology and people skills to ensure that the business culture remains functional and promotes positive behaviours.

Bias management systems and controls

Cognitive bias	Application	Everyday examples	Influence norm strategy
Overconfidence, planning fallacy, hindsight	Underestimation of risk/size of task, over-optimism and 'selective memory' – which we all suffer from with the human condition engineered to be over-optimistic, in control and to think we know more than we actually do	Ability to pay off loans, mistaking return luck for skill, overtrading, overwhelmed by information, lack of seeking council	Employing third-party professionals (eg NEDs) to take a step back and give a reasoned view, applying risk-management tech to ensure strategies are modelled and risks identified, monitored and managed
Inertia, procrastination, willpower	Instant gratification, pain avoidance, fear and distress, industry noise and time out of a market can lead to immobilisation	Taking the path of least resistance, 'learned' pessimism	Simplification, autopilot nudge schemes such as auto-enrolment pensions (eg Nest), salience and social proof in evidencing significant other proactive behaviours
Status quo	Change aversion and hyperbolic discounting where short termism is favoured, discounting long-term over short-term benefits	Attraction to service or product inducements, endowment effect, valuing goods more when owned than when not	A 'lock-in' approach to contract remuneration based on client satisfaction, AI that models analytics for long-term benefits of business strategies

Cognitive dissonance	Embarrassment and buyer's remorse	Taking on too much debt, buying products on emotion only	Counter-intuitive strategy, sleeping on decisions, applying Monte Carlo modelling to identify outlier decision-making against the culturally aligned norm
Loss and regret aversion	Endowment and myopic effect, unhealthy appetite for risk	Holding poor performing funds and selling winners	Employing professional third parties and tech for risk, research and governance management
Groupthink	Coalescence around poor decision-making	Excessively optimistic about own skills, knowledge, power and moral coding	Diversified board and NEDs, diagnostics to assess effects of decision-making, using ESN tech to collate the teams' views
Mental accounting	Hedonic editing, segmenting attractive investment from debt or loss	Income favoured over long-term business worth	Using KPI diagnostics and trend analysis across budget planning, accounting and cash flows

(Continued)

(Cont)

Cognitive bias	Application	Everyday examples	Influence norm strategy
Shortcuts, deviant decision-making, narrow framing	Affect heuristics, rules of thumb, experiential memory projection, acting without considering all the implications	Ignoring risk-return profiling and taking a simplistic approach by investing in the familiar, investing on market sentiment, allowing groupthink to dominate	Employing algorithms to model big picture 'unknown unknown' strategies against what is known, introducing moral coding and enhancing accountabilities via a code of conduct
Information misuse, anchoring effect	Anchoring effect, prices and costs are set in context and superficial decision-making, stereotyping, emotional contagion	Past business performance indicates future gains, irrational fear on market pricing, following the herd mentality	Restricting news and industry noise exposure, recognition of emotionally laden judgements via EQ strategies
Herding	Copying the behaviour of others, going with the crowd	Investment based on tips from friends or following fashionable strategy, selling in sheer panic	Taking a counter-intuitive approach, employing expert third parties and tech that can forecast multiple financial strategies
Escalation, sunk cost	Throwing good money after bad	Investing into a losing investment despite size of loss	Employing tech to actively ignore price and market fluctuations

I am no fan of taking a silo strategy to bias diagnosis and management, but it is helpful to review the types of bias that can play out in organisations and the people strategy and technology tools that can be used to better manage or control both bias and noise and promote a healthy, collaborate culture.

Chapter checkpoints

- Build your systems around a healthy GRC structure. It's a bit like a football team: any great team will have their foundations securely recruited through the 'spine' of the team – ie the defence, midfield and attack. You need to ensure your systems and controls create the right choice architecture to encourage the right decision-making and behaviour to meet ongoing goals and objectives.

- As behavioural biases can affect individual decision-making, apply moral coding and the fight technology to de-bias decision-making. This can provide the foundations and spine for your business to flourish. Ensure staff have the right incentives, encourage culture careers and put moral coding in place so you can encourage and publicise examples of good behaviour.

- As the 'availability heuristic' is likely to affect people's behaviour, so make your systems and controls salient. This will give you the best chance for developing your desired constructive culture.

- Employ the bias management table. It can provide a big advantage for the cyber strategy I advocate, in navigating an individual's unconscious bias by applying third-party technologies and their algorithms to help manage the risk of making the wrong decisions.

- Keep it simple: focus on one to three technology and AI applications that can scale your services quickly, securely and effectively.

NINE
Your Promise

We've all heard of well-known brand names filing for bankruptcy after discounting competitors who have adopted digital products, and online shopping platforms doing away with high street brands. What these businesses had in common was the fact that they were unable to change or spot services their customers were switching to quickly enough to survive. With an NRE empowered by a digital revolution, businesses need to take a long hard look at their service propositions as well as their products to ensure they are sustainable going forward.

Pretty obvious, I know, but I can't emphasis enough that it is those businesses that have the right team, with high business EQ and client relationship capital, and employ the right technologies who will be able to take full advantage of the NRE and formulate flexible service propositions. We know that customers now expect subscription experiences with ongoing value – memorable experiences with immediate fulfilment, available any time, anywhere, and full of personalised moments. When we bring service propositions into the equation, we can add the fact that a tailored service which makes it easy for customers to understand and buy is essential.

Data analytics and your service proposition

One of the best services I have witnessed is the video streaming platforms and their film and television streaming services. It is revolutionary to devise a system based around ad-free, bingeworthy content tailored to customers' preferences and, yes, biases. Considering how little time it has taken for streaming platforms to gain popularity, they have stacked up heaps of data about their viewers, including their age, gender, location and taste in media. By gathering information across every customer interaction, these streaming models can dive right into the minds of their viewers and get an idea of what they might like to watch next even before they finish a show or movie.

Now this is clever, very clever, as individual choice is important in the NRE, and it is those businesses that can collate and scrutinise data to understand what their customers crave that can then design their services around those wants to ensure a sticky service that tailors its content to encourage deep and sustainable customer engagement. One of the latest streaming developments hosts consumer news about renewals, release dates and extra content, all designed to immerse consumers in their ongoing experience and for algorithms to further understand their preferences.

These digital streaming platforms use metrics such as: what day and time customers watch, the devices they use, the nature of the content, their searches on the platform, excerpts that are rewatched, whether content was paused, rewound or fast-forwarded, user location, when content is left, any ratings provided, and browsing and scrolling behaviours. This data is then used to develop algorithms and generate critical insights that provide real-time recommendations and help steer the company in the right direction.

Just think about the potential for data science in your business. If you haven't already, I would highly recommend you start to explore how data analytics could help personalise the services and products you provide.

Of course all this comes with the need to engage ethics and moral coding within our relevant industries. In the financial services, there are strict regulations and directives to comply with to ensure the customer gains services that are suitable for their short- to long-term needs. One way industry can pull together to ensure morality and ethics are at the centre of their services and activities is engaging society in a responsible way.

CASE STUDY: Capital Asset Management

Our company culture is based around our five core values, or the 'five Cs': client-centred, collaborative, creative, curious and candid.

Every six months, we ask our team to complete an anonymous online engagement survey, which assesses how we are all feeling about our purpose, the company, our leaders, us as individuals and our customers. There is the facility to provide anonymous free-typed feedback in each section, and we offer objective scoring. The output report groups comments and provides our operations team with steer in terms of where upcoming projects need to focus.

Key to our culture and the delivery of our business plan is a recently adopted platform for monitoring objectives and key results (OKRs). The company vision, mission, annual objectives and individual objectives are logged on this system – including key results – so we have a clear idea of what 'done' looks like and by when.

There is the facility to do weekly check-ins to update on progress and confidence levels relating to your objectives. The other benefit of the software is that we can log in and see everyone's OKRs, so if we want an update on progress, we can easily find it.

Corporate social responsibility

CSR has been around for a long time. In the 1880s the Quakers introduced a system for caring for others through corporate communities, which led to the birth of what are called 'mutual societies', such as building societies, credit unions or friendly societies. What we are now witnessing is a new age for ESG within financial services regulation, which is based around ensuring investment and investment businesses offer the opportunity to align investment and CSR values.

It is important to model your principles in CSR and ensure you have client ESG at the heart of your service propositions. With research showing that up to 80% of consumers are more likely to purchase a product labelled environmentally friendly and 77% (mainly millennials) concerned at the environmental impact of the products they buy, you cannot ignore CSR within your promise.[74]

Again data analytics will help here. By assessing what is important to your clients and your staff, you will begin to influence and align their behaviour with your desired culture. Remember the underlying levels for cultural growth: preferences, beliefs, habits, behaviours and values. By aligning or re-aligning these layers you will attract the right stakeholders (including customers) to your business as you develop and grow, fulfilling your stakeholders' beliefs and values. The trick is to ensure this corporate culture promotes CSR at all times.

Research has illustrated the CSR performance is statistically significant in business economic value and innovation. CSR brings diversity, higher employee and community engagement and environmental benefits. It can also help lower financing costs and provide competitive differentiation with customers attracted to companies that are committed to CSR.

The latest regulatory directive within financial services can help break this down. ESG provides a framework for your company to evidence its commitment to sustainable responsibility. You can benchmark your service proposition and general business practices against various metrics, such as:

- **Environmental:** Policies, emissions, energy management, renewables, outsourcing

- **Social:** Employee wellbeing, D&I, employee engagement, health and safety, community engagement, product responsibility

- **Governance:** Ethics and morality, board diversity, remuneration, risk management, data security, supply chain management

There is evidence of a strong correlation between CSR and sustainable, profitable business. Research shows that technology companies that spend more on CSR experience a corresponding increase in revenue and profitability. Why is this? It is clear that building a strong ESG strategy incorporating a responsible business, clear values and a focus on 'people over profit' attracts dynamic talent and allows the business to align its innovative approach with building goodwill with governments, stakeholders, employees and customers.

One prominent video streaming service offers fifty-two weeks of paid parental leave (compared to a median of eighteen weeks at other regtech companies). One social media business seems to have taken the circular economy (the sixth factor of our NRE) to heart in designing servers from the ground up to last longer, recycling components from old servers into new ones and selling old servers on the secondary market. As a result of these initiatives alone, they have become one of the companies with the lowest staff turnover and this has led the way in increasing the number of remanufactured units selling over 2 million machines each year.

Service segmentation

In Chapter Six we discussed the importance of segmentation when it comes to customer engagement. To limit cognitive biases and their potential detrimental effect on human decision-making, it is imperative that firms align their products and services with their customers' needs. This means gaining a firm understanding of customers' behavioural preferences and commercial consumption needs.

If the NRE is ignored, then you will only gain a one-dimensional understanding of your customers' needs. This can generally be viewed as a transactional relationship, which is shallow and ad hoc in nature. What is required is a partnership and holistic approach to understanding what exactly your clients' propensities to purchase your products and services are. As we have seen from the video streaming model, technology can help enormously: algorithms can be designed to assess their customers' personal preferences and deliver tailored products to meet them.

This is also evident in the success of leading online shopping platforms in assessing online consumer behaviour to fine-tune their recommendations. Some of these platforms employ 'smart assistants' to assess customer behaviour by 'listening' to their owners and sending data to the online platform so the system can offer products that are segmented to their clients' needs. It is important to mention that owners can take control over their smart assistants and online cookie management and turn off data collection features.

Technology and service segmentation can be a potent alliance for good. Within my industry, client segmentation is a regulatory requirement, so clients and customers may receive service and product features and benefits that are appropriate and suitable to meet their ongoing needs. As the table below illustrates, it is deemed good practice for wealth management firms to segment not only by financial needs but also by behavioural needs too.

Retail financial services client bank segmentation strategy

Segment	Subsegment	Investment solution	Platform selection	Advisory service	Review service	Clients in vulnerable circumstances	Cost £ Initial	PA
Young accumulators	Job starters	Savings account, Lifetime Individual Savings Account (LISA)	Simple low cost	Light touch, tech, sustainability	1 × pa			
	Young execs	Individual Savings Account (ISA)	Discretionary Fund Management (DFM)	Standard, tech, sustainability	1 × pa			
Runway to retirement	Employed	Defined Contribution, auto-enrolment	Model portfolio Discretionary	Standard, advanced, sustainability	1 × pa			
	Self-employed	Personal Pension Plan (PPP)	Centralised Investment Proposition (CIP)	Light/standard, sustainability	2 × pa			
Retirement income	Low/no income	Centralised Retirement Proposition (CRP)	Invest/annuity	Standard, sustainability	2 × pa			
	High income	Growth	Invest/withdrawal	Cash flow/ bespoke, sustainability	2 × pa			
Outliers					1 × pa			
Vulnerable	Mental, physical	Protected	Invest/withdrawal	Tailored sustainability	3 × pa			

Segmentation of services and products can also increase profitability. In essence, engaging the NRE via a streamlined and segmented service with tailored products can provide specialised services, which means the offerings can be lucrative. If you have employed technology to enable this strategy, then costs can be kept lower, and the segmented services will be far more sustainable and efficient.

For a 'people-dependent' business model (for example consultancy, accountants or lawyers), revenues will be higher to maintain the personnel to enable these services. By leveraging the power of algorithm-driven automation and data analytics to 'productise' aspects of work, innovative firms are finding margins can be increased while they provide customers with better and more personalised services. This can mean rising productivity and efficiency, and scaling business strategy as streamlined services take over high-volume tasks and aid judgement-driven processes. This all frees up staff time to focus on more sophisticated tasks and generate greater value for the company.

By using technology to streamline segmentation and personalise services, firms can ensure they build a customer-focused culture and aid better decision-making through services and products suited to customers' needs and objectives.

The client value proposition

If you want to be a true client-centric business, then your charging structure and strategy needs to start with your client journey. As you can see from the above table, if you segment your clients into comparable characteristics and journeys, you can then also ensure you tailor your costs, charges and fees around their needs and objectives.

By mapping your client needs and objectives and your business's products and services, and measuring client engagement along the way, you can understand your value proposition: one that clients highly value, that provides engineered outputs tailored to the client's ongoing needs, evidences good outcomes and encourages client loyalty, and thus will continue to pay your fees and charges without question. We call this the client lifetime value (CLV): your cash flow ÷ your client loyalty rate = your cost of business operations.

Your CLV is enhanced significantly if efficient technology enables your clients to experience high value. Remember, in this new relationship-based economy of high personalisation, if business can make it easy for clients to gain instant gratification and educate them quickly on the benefits of the product and service, this will drive a high value proposition and sticky client relationships.

Client noise and bias

In a 2023 survey of 3,000 global CEOs, the highest-performing leaders cited competitive advantage as dependent on who has the most advanced generative AI, yet when executives discuss how to do better in client engagement, they often fail to recognise that customer–employee interactions are vulnerable to bias.[75] In 2018, for example, a Starbucks manager summoned police to arrest two black men who hadn't ordered anything; the manager assumed they were loitering, but they were merely waiting for an acquaintance.

It is important when designing and operating customer service propositions that you manage your own staff and your customer biases as best you can in an ethical way. If they are not addressed, then this can be fatal for your business. Why? It's the NRE stupid (not you, just a play on Bill Clinton's 'It's the Economy Stupid' 1992 election strapline). In the digital age, social media provides too much of an opportunity for customers to post negative or positive reviews about their consumer experiences. A firm's reputation can be damaged (fairly or unfairly) by one far-reaching social media post.

As this book is heavily focused on technology and how this can enable constructive culture, if your firm has deployed technology to gain data on customer behaviour and their demographic characteristics, then you have a good chance of identifying where bias might exist in your customer service proposition(s).

As we have seen, customer surveys and segmentation are also a good way of gaining valuable data to assess people's sensitivities to product and/or service features, costs and charges, and propensities to purchase certain products and/or services. If you have data analytics that will gain trend analysis on your customers, you have valuable MI that can point to areas where bias may be hindering services or products your customers are demanding. This could be due to the customer's age; for example, older customers may have to wait longer to receive your service, perhaps because they are not comfortable with the type of technology you are using to distribute services.

By collating the right data across all customer segments, you will ensure that any internal staff or external customer biases can be identified and managed. Experimentation can also help here: trialling what does and does not work can be invaluable in assessing the customer experience.

Other, more common, techniques include focus groups, mystery shopping (hiring shoppers from different demographic groups to interact with customer service employees) and creating control groups, where one group is set to normal procedures and does not include something being tested and another experimental group does. Examples of these are abundant in the digital world.

Addressing bias incorporates diagnosis and some of the technologies we have already discussed in this book can help here. Using the social enterprise network platform to gain data on customer relationship issues and what is and is not working, and assessing customer behaviour through service and product engagement can all provide valuable MI on where customer bias lies and how to deal with it. Examples of how business can use techniques to influence clients ethically include:

- **Loss aversion:** As Daniel Kahneman put it, we feel the pain of loss far more than the thrill of a gain. If a brand manages to convince consumers that by not buying a particular product they are likely to lose out on something, it can successfully manage to achieve higher sales.

- **Social proof:** If humans can find evidence that their choice is a good one, then this can help justify the purchase.

- **Framing effect:** This all depends on the way the product or price points are presented.

- **Anchoring:** This depends on how the information is presented against a particular reference point.

- **Confirmation:** New information confirms pre-existing beliefs, known as rules of thumb or heuristics – eg if a brand can affirm clients' expectations.

- **Herding and 'bandwagon' effect:** Linked to social proof, this suggests clients will purchase if others do too.

- **Salience:** Using stand-out features that engage clients' immediate needs is a powerful strategy.

- **Zero risk:** Customers will be attracted to products or services that appear to mitigate any risks. Overconfidence bias also plays a part here in overestimating zero risk.

- **Exposure effect:** High visibility of a product or service can trigger a view that it is popular and lead to a positive purchase decision.

Decision prosthetics and changing the choice architecture

If you are into your behavioural economics, then you may well have read Robert Thaler and Cass Sunstein's acclaimed book, *Nudge*,[76] which takes a libertarian, paternalist approach to nudging people to make better life choices, such as automatic enrolment in a pension with an opt-out (most stay invested) or the use of default options and changing the information people are provided with. This makes the system personal and easy to understand and relate to; for example, utility bills with the individual's energy use compared to the area's average, which can encourage energy and money savings.

On its own, nudge can be a limited tool and does not always deliver the desired results, and it may not be helpful in encouraging confident decision-making in complex environments, such as businesses. Some may view libertarian paternalism as an afront to free choice, so technology and algorithms can help when it comes to clients engaging with products and services.

Firstly, by designing holistic systems and information, such as management for any risk of service or product purchase, an algorithm could present information regarding the implications and interrelated aspects to help individuals manage any complexities. Examples are:

- **Gamification:** To encourage easy, comfortable and enjoyable engagement with complex systems

- **Planning systems:** To help clients think about, schedule and bundle decisions, reducing engagement points and any emotional discomfort with making immediate decisions

- **Education:** Delivered to manage saliency at the point of the decision-making process, so clients take note and are well informed

- **Decision supports:** To encourage feedback and respond to buyer behaviours

Secondly, personalisation encourages engagement and trust in business products and services. Examples are:

- **Life-moments:** Ensuring CRM technology has the client's birthday and other important life events to provide tailored communications

- **Tailored products and services:** Personalised to the client's situation and ongoing needs, data can be used to offer targeted defaults as opposed to one-size-fits-all defaults

Thirdly, choice architecture should be designed for engagement and action. Examples are:

- **Compelling choices:** Offering products around stated client goals, such as retirement or holiday plans
- **Simplified processes:** Clear options that can manage client inertia

Buyer behaviour can be complex, and businesses also need to be aware of any unintended consequences their services and products can create. One strategy that most businesses would benefit from is randomised control trials that thoroughly test propositions to encourage engagement and assess what works and what does not, as well as determining whether buyer behaviour and the way services and products are sold and perform are leading to good or poor outcomes and client detriment.

By using both human and technology intervention in the choice architecture and ongoing client journey, you can better manage emotionally laden judgements for both your business and your clients and evidence good client outcomes and satisfaction with the services and products purchased.

Chapter checkpoints

- Employ data analytics. You will not regret it as it will provide invaluable trend, gap and root cause analysis and evidence for changes and strategy to grow.

- Use the universal principal of reciprocity and employ CSR with causes that are close to you and your staff and clients.

- Use algorithms to aid better decision-making across the business and with your clients and employ decision prosthetics to support positive and functional decision-making.

- Reimagine how your business can look and feel with technology and AI at the heart of its products, services, systems and controls.

Conclusion

Writing a book is no mean feat, and finishing it is also hard: how do you bring all these ideas, learnings and experiences together in a meaningful way? Well, the driver behind this book is developing and implementing a technology-focused framework that can empower your culture and provide sustainable business performance.

The five culture code keys we have devised are currently helping over a thousand firms find their way around relevant regulations and automate their diagnostic gap analysis and audit processes, so they have all the data and MI they need in real time, as well as resources to evidence GRC, reducing compliance time and costs along the way. We have found these keys are universal in their application across business practice, no matter which industry and market firms operate in.

The NRE demands firms implement a culture code, and the five keys provide a culture code that allows you to build a road map to ensure your clients' needs are met at all times, staff are engaged, and the business operations are resilient, effective and efficient – all supporting sustainable performance.

Aligning your business to culture coding values

As with any change, your business needs to buy in to the NRE, and in the age of personalisation change can be difficult, but if you employ the strategies listed in our five key areas, and embed appropriate technology and organisational behaviour strategies across the business proposition, then you stand a good chance of benefitting from the culture coding framework.

Whether you are a start-up, SME or larger, when applying technology to your business model it is important to take a holistic view and avoid tick boxes and checklists as you plan and then implement technology that integrates and enables you to grow ethically and sustainably.

There are so many tools out there that firms can suffer from overwhelm. Using the culture coding framework and strategies in this book will help your firm identify suitable third-party technology and AI – or, indeed, to develop your own that can support your business growth in the new relationship economy.

Employing OSS is central to your business remaining agile, flexible, innovative, competitive and relevant to your changing client and business needs. It will also ensure that the principle of culture coding is embedded in your business culture. OSS will enable data and MI to flow securely across the five keys and allow other third parties to use your technology easily and effectively if this is part of your business model.

Data is the glue

The digital revolution has brought into hard focus the need for firms to collect, scrutinise and present high-quality data. Where culture coding and technology are concerned, data is the glue that binds the five keys together so firms have a bedrock of EBP and MI that can be called upon 24/7 and used to guide them through challenges and opportunities that will always arise in their respective markets.

Data analytics across the five keys will provide you with all the trend and gap analysis necessary to ensure you continuously improve and have the ability to communicate clearly and with gravitas with all stakeholders regarding services, products and overall performance. Also remember the marginal gains approach: by applying this and measuring results via technology, your business can increase and sustain ongoing profits and performance. This is crucial when it comes to key areas that start-ups and SMEs face when fundraising.

Fundraising and culture coding

'Welcome to the lion's den!' That was what I was greeted with on my first pitch for seed funding back in 2019. For start-ups, in particular, this can be incredibly challenging and, yes, demoralising if you are doing the angel investor or venture capital rounds. The key to gaining attention and standing out in the crowd is presenting your culture code. A pitch deck is all about reassuring potential investors that you have done your homework, have a viable proposition within your market, traction can be quick and the model is scalable. Your pitch deck should offer a catchy and comprehensive review of the five keys and a good grasp on financials, such as projected turnover and profits.

Guy Kawasaki, who has written many impressive business books, including *The Art of the Start 2.0* and *Enchantment*,[77] has a great nine-step pitch framework which incorporates many of the five culture code keys:

1. **Problem/opportunity:** Describe the pain you are alleviating or the pleasure you are providing. Use your focus key where your mission and vision statements should address this.

2. **Value proposition:** Your engagement and your promise will help you explain the value of the pain you alleviate or the pleasure provided.

3. **The magic:** Your promise will describe the technology behind your service and/or product.

4. **Business model:** Your focus should explain how you will gain market growth, your metrics and scalability.

5. **Go-to-market plan:** Your engagement should show how you will reach your clients.

6. **Competitive analysis:** Your focus and your promise should provide a comprehensive view of the competition.

7. **The team:** Your people will detail who are the key members across directors, advisers and any investors.

8. **Financial forecast:** Your focus should provide a five-to-ten-year forecast. If you are a young business then this could be a discounted cash flow focusing on future income which, as Peter Thiel explains in his excellent book *Zero to One*,[78] is effectively how most technology businesses gain investment interest.

9. **Timeline of accomplishments and use of funds:** All five keys will document your journey key wins, your pipeline and what you are planning.

Developing a cyber approach

One of the key challenges I have had in designing and launching a regtech platform is that it is initially viewed as competition and a disrupter to compliance officers' positions. This is not the case, and it has taken plenty of education, webinars and conferences to allay these fears.

AI could well replace some jobs over the coming years, but the issue is that technology and AI can also make existing individuals more effective and competent in their roles, rather than replacing them. We talk about taking a 'cyber compliance' view on our regtech and the same should be applied to your business plan and propositions.

If you are engaging in the NRE, then it is wise to ensure you have your technology focused on the EQ framework I detailed in Chapter Three and the client segmentation strategies in Chapters Six and Nine. This means that not every service or proposition needs to be completely digitised, but there are those that may well benefit from being 100% digital. It is important to analyse your client and staff behaviours against desired strategic outcomes so you can then work out where technology should be employed as an enabler rather than a replacement to human performance.

This 'cyber approach' means either building or adopting third-party technology that can make existing activities more efficient and effective, gain more data and MI, and ensure staff are well trained to use it so clients gain maximum benefits. If your business model is B2C then there may well be a case for employing technology only to better serve your clients, so, again, careful due diligence needs to be taken, as discussed in Chapter One.

What I have found is that by employing empathy, placing yourself in your staff's and clients' shoes, you will gain a more granular understanding of what technology is appropriate to meet ongoing needs and balance the human and technology application and activities across your proposition.

Innovation is key

As can be seen in our case studies, it is those firms who have conducted their research and due diligence on the need for applying or building technology to meet a need, either within their organisation or for the market in general, who succeed the most.

If you wish to apply technology within your business, you will obviously need to assess any incumbent (or legacy) technology and review whether this is fit for purpose going forward. We have seen examples of businesses going bust or severely impairing their ability to remain profitable because they have not conducted enough research around replacing existing technology or have just stuck with what they have rather than twist.

AI is receiving plenty of attention presently, good and bad, but there is no escaping the fact that we need to engage AI if we are to enjoy the benefits it can bring to our business and client needs. Not only will generative AI streamline business operations, compliance, client services and much more, it will also create new careers that need human soft skills and emotional intelligence.

The NRE in which we now operate demands high personalisation and instant gratification for information. This also goes with regulators and governmental bodies who set the rules and regulations. They need real-time data and MI to ensure markets remain stable and competitive and dysfunctions are ironed out fast.

Engaging organisational behaviour strategies

When studying for my MSc in organisational behaviour, it was apparent that across key topics and business strategies, such as technology, employee wellbeing, training and development, statistics, client engagement and leadership, unconscious bias is a major fly in the ointment where constructive culture is concerned.

Applying the five culture coding keys is helpful if you wish to root out dysfunctional decision-making, bias and behaviours along with applying emotional intelligence to your leadership, team and client engagement strategies. As we have seen, using the right technology, such as social enterprise platforms and/or CRMs, will enable your business to identify those culture carriers who will bring the right competence and conduct to the organisation and drive a positive culture.

This also means embedding governance and risk oversight from the top down and making sure communications, responsibilities and accountabilities are clear, understood and followed through with EBP at the heart of all decision-making.

The culture coding matrix

'If you cannot measure it, you cannot improve it,' the old business strategy mantra says. Where technology and data are concerned, as we have seen through EBP, built and used well with open sourcing they can deliver a 'single source of truth' that shines a light across the five culture coding keys, proving a business is on the right course in serving their mission, clients and stakeholders (or not). The below culture coding matrix shows that if firms apply these principles, they will gain a highly relational and transformational culture.

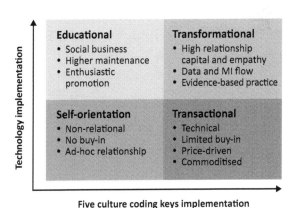

Culture coding matrix

Final thoughts

As mentioned in my introduction, this book is an amalgamation of thirty years of experience across different guises within the retail financial services industry. The aim is to pull relevant strategy from this experience that could help you, in whatever shape or form, as you build your business in this digital age.

The NRE is an opportunity to re-assess and calibrate your business position and strategy and evaluate what technology could now help you attract and retain the right staff and clients and ensure you become a scalable and investable commodity in your own right. There are no right or wrong answers or activities, and I am sure you will have your own ideas, yet the culture coding philosophy I employ can provide a meaningful framework for you to sense check your business, revisiting areas you have already considered or new ones that you may have just not had the time to address.

Culture coding is all about remaining open to the concept of technology as an enabler. It is also about not rushing into action but taking careful steps so you do not upset your current business model, and applying any or all of the five keys and their strategies on a staged basis to gain a digitally focused business and constructive culture. Rome was not built in a day and nor is business success, but if you employ your EQ, remain open to technology and AI as a way to add efficiency, evidence and agility to your existing business model, this will place you in a positive position to grow and thrive in this NRE.

I wish you well on your culture coding journey.

Notes

1   National Science Foundation, 'Evidence of earliest known domestic horses found in Kazakhstan' (5 March 2009), www.nsf.gov/news/news_summ.jsp?cntn_id=114345, accessed 6 June 2023

2   L Hurst, 'OpenAI says 80% of workers could see their jobs impacted by AI. These are the jobs most affected', Euronews (30 March 2023), www.euronews.com/next/2023/03/23/openai-says-80-of-workers-could-see-their-jobs-impacted-by-ai-these-are-the-jobs-most-affe, accessed 11 July 2023

3   RM Yerkes and JD Dodson, 'The relation of strength of stimulus to rapidity of habit-formation', *Journal of Comparative Neurology and Psychology*, 18 (1908), 459–482

4   *2022 Job Seeker Nation Report* (Jobvite, 2022), www.jobvite.com/lp/2022-job-seeker-nation-report, accessed 11 July 2023

5   D Drennan, *Transforming Company Culture* (McGraw-Hill, 1992)

6   E Schein, *Organizational Culture and Leadership* (Wiley Press, 2004)

7   G Hofstede, *Culture's Consequences: Comparing values, behaviors, institutions and organizations across nations* (2nd edn, Sage Publications, 1984)

8   Ibid

9   D Kahneman, JL Knetsch, RH Thaler, 'Anomalies: The
    endowment effect, loss aversion, and status quo bias', *The
    Journal of Economic Perspectives*, 5/1 (1991), 193–206, www.
    aeaweb.org/articles?id=10.1257/jep.5.1.193, accessed
    6 June 2023

10 MI Norton, D Mochon, D Ariely, 'The IKEA effect: When
    labor leads to love', *Journal of Consumer Psychology*,
    22/3 (July 2012), 453–460, https://dash.harvard.edu/
    handle/1/12136084, accessed 11 July 2023

11 US Secretary of Defense, Donald Rumsfeld, 2002 press
    briefing transcript, www.nato.int/docu/speech/2002/
    s020606g.htm, accessed 11 July 2023

12 Communication Theory, 'The Johari Window Model',
    www.communicationtheory.org/the-johari-window-model,
    accessed 8 June 2023

13 D Kahneman, O Sibony, C Sunstein, *Noise: A flaw in human
    judgment* (William Collins, 2021)

14 RF Baumeister, *Willpower: Why self-control is the secret to
    success* (Penguin books, 2009)

15 SL Beilock and TH Carr, 'When high-powered people fail:
    Working memory and "choking under pressure" in math',
    Psychological Science, 16/2 (February 2005), 101–105, www.
    jstor.org/stable/40064185, accessed 7 June 2023

16 A Bandura, *Self-efficacy: The exercise of control* (Worth
    Publishers, 1997)

17 F Herzberg, 'One more time: How do you motivate
    employees?', *Harvard Business Review* (1968), https://qi.elft.
    nhs.uk/wp-content/uploads/2015/12/9-herzberg.pdf,
    accessed 7 June 2023

18 AH Maslow, 'A theory of human motivation', *Psychological
    Review*, 50 (1943), 370–396, https://psychclassics.yorku.ca/
    Maslow/motivation.htm, accessed 7 June 2023

19 D Ariely, 'What's the value of a big bonus?', *New York Times*
    (2008), www.nytimes.com/2008/11/20/opinion/20ariely.
    html, accessed 7 June 2023

20 S Hegarty, 'The boss who put everyone on 70K' (BBC
    News, 28 February 2020), www.bbc.co.uk/news/
    stories-51332811, accessed 7 June 2023

21 D Kahneman and A Deaton, 'High income improves
    evaluation of life but not emotional well-being',
    Psychological and Cognitive Sciences, 107/38 (2010), 16489–

16493, www.pnas.org/doi/10.1073/pnas.1011492107#tab-citations, accessed 11 July 2023

22 DH Pink, *To Sell Is Human* (Canongate Books, 2013)

23 D Goleman, *Emotional Intelligence: Why it can matter more than IQ* (Bloomsbury, 1995)

24 Hay Group, *Engage Employees and Boost Performance* (2021), https://home.ubalt.edu/tmitch/642/Articles%20syllabus/Hay%20assoc%20engaged_performance_120401.pdf, accessed 7 June 2023

25 LJ Peter and R Hull, *The Peter Principle: Why things always go wrong* (Profile Books, 2020)

26 HA Simon, 'What is an "explanation" of behavior?' In: P Thagard, ed, *Mind Readings: Introductory selections on cognitive science* (Cognet, 1998), pp1–28

27 C Woodward, *How to Win* (Hodder & Stoughton, 2019)

28 R Moore, *How Dave Brailsford Reinvented the Wheel* (Backpage Press, 2013)

29 DM Rousseau and BC Gunia, 'Evidence-based practice: The psychology of EBP implementation', *Annual Review of Psychology*, 67 (2016), 667–692, https://pubmed.ncbi.nlm.nih.gov/26361048, accessed 11 July 2023

30 C Davies, *Winning Client Trust: The Retail Distribution Review and the UK financial services industry's battle for its clients' hearts and minds* (Ecademy Press, 2011)

31 W Childs, '1492–1494: Columbus and the discovery of America', *Economic History Review*, 48/4 (1995), 754–768, www.jstor.org/stable/2598134, accessed 11 July 2023

32 ME Porter, *On Competition: Updated and expanded edition* (Harvard Business Review Press, 2008)

33 Ellen MacArthur Foundation, *Artificial Intelligence and the Circular Economy* (2019), https://ellenmacarthurfoundation.org/artificial-intelligence-and-the-circular-economy, accessed 7 June 2023

34 S Covey, *The 7 Habits of Highly Effective People* (Simon & Schuster, 2007)

35 M Syed, *Rebel Ideas* (John Murray Publishers, 2020)

36 J Aguilar, *Scanning the Business Environment* (Macmillan, 1967)

37 A Thackray, *Moore's Law: The life of Gordon Moore, Silicon Valley's quiet revolutionary* (Basic Books, 2015)

38 A Bhattacharya, N Lang and J Hemerling, *Beyond Great: Nine strategies for thriving in an era of social tension, economic*

nationalism, and technological revolution (Nicholas Brealey Publishing, 2021)

39   C Woodward, 'Speaking services' (no date), www.clivewoodward.com/speaking, accessed 26 June 2023

40   D Maister, C Green, R Galford, *The Trusted Advisor* (Simon & Schuster, 2002)

41   D Lambert and K Dugdale, *Smarter Selling: How to grow sales by building trusted relationships* (Financial Times, 2011)

42   M Dixon, K Freeman, N Toman, 'Stop trying to delight your customers', *Harvard Business Review* (July–August 2010), https://hbr.org/2010/07/stop-trying-to-delight-your-customers, accessed 10 July 2023

43   Ibid

44   R Kaplan and D Norton, 'The balanced scorecard: Measures that drive performance', *Harvard Business Review* (January–February 1992), https://hbr.org/1992/01/the-balanced-scorecard-measures-that-drive-performance-2, accessed 11 July 2023; ME Porter, *On Competition: Updated and expanded edition* (Harvard Business Review Press, 2008)

45   *The Great Wealth Transfer* (Engage Insight Consultancy, 2018), http://engageinsight.co.uk/great-wealth-transfer, accessed 10 August 2023

46   D Levitin, *The Organized Mind: Thinking straight in the age of information overload* (Penguin, 2015)

47   J Lehrer, *Imagine: How creativity works* (Houghton Mifflin Harcourt, 2012)

48   Washington Center for Women's and Children's Wellness, 'The benefits of napping' (no date), www.wcwcw.org/blog/the-benefits-of-napping, accessed 15 June 2023

49   D Kahneman, O Sibony, C Sunstein, *Noise: A flaw in human judgment* (William Collins, 2021)

50   A Bhattacharya, N Lang and J Hemerling, *Beyond Great: Nine strategies for thriving in an era of social tension, economic nationalism, and technological revolution* (Nicholas Brealey Publishing, 2021)

51   R Kelley, 'In praise of followers', *Harvard Business Review* (1988), https://hbr.org/1988/11/in-praise-of-followers, accessed 7 June 2023

52   J Collins and J Porras, *Built to Last: Successful habits of visionary companies* (Random House, 2005)

53   Gallup, *State of the Global Workplace: 2023 report* (2023), www.gallup.com/workplace/349484/state-of-the-global-workplace.aspx, accessed 11 July 2023

54 VE Horigian, DR Schmidt, DJ Feaster, 'Loneliness, mental health, and substance use among US young adults during COVID-19', *Journal of Psychoactive Drugs*, 53/1 (2021), 1–9, https://doi.org/10.1080/02791072.2020.1836435

55 L Feldman Barrett and J Russell, 'Independence and bipolarity in the structure of current affect', *Journal of Personality and Social Psychology*, 74/4 (1998), 967–984, https://doi.org/10.1037/0022-3514.74.4.967

56 Ibid

57 VH Vroom, *Work and Motivation* (Wiley, 1994)

58 M Csikszentmihalyi, *Flow: The psychology of optimal experience* (Harper and Rowe, 1990)

59 M Gladwell, *Outliers* (Penguin, 2009)

60 M Csikszentmihalyi, *Flow: The psychology of optimal experience* (Harper and Rowe, 1990)

61 Ibid

62 C Newport, *Deep Work: Rules for focused success in a distracted world* (Grand Central Publishing, 2016)

63 C Wilson Meloncelli, 'The Autotelic personality: Finding happiness in flow' (Hack the Flow State, no date), www.cwilsonmeloncelli.com/the-autotelic-personality-finding-happiness-in-flow, accessed 13 June 2023

64 D Ariely, *The Honest Truth About Dishonesty* (HarperCollins, 2010)

65 Financial Reporting Council, *Board Diversity and Effectiveness in FTSE 350 Companies* (FRC, 2021), www.frc.org.uk/getattachment/3cc05eae-2024-45d8-b14c-abb2ac7497aa/FRC-Board-Diversity-and-Effectiveness-in-FTSE-350-Companies.pdf, accessed 11 July 2023

66 Financial Conduct Authority, *Diversity and Inclusion on Company Boards and Executive Management: Policy Statement PS22/3* (FCA, 2022), www.fca.org.uk/publications/policy-statements/ps22-3-diversity-inclusion-company-boards-executive-managment, accessed July 2023

67 A Turing, *Computing Machinery and Intelligence* (Blackwell for the Mind Association, 1950)

68 S Russell and P Norvig, *Artificial Intelligence: A modern approach* (Pearson, 2016)

69 D Kahneman, O Sibony, C Sunstein, *Noise: A flaw in human judgment* (William Collins, 2021)

70 Bank of England and FCA, *Machine Learning in UK Financial Services* (2019), www.bankofengland.co.uk/report/2019/

machine-learning-in-uk-financial-services, accessed
7 June 2023

71   M Ford, *The Lights in the Tunnel* (CreateSpace, 2009); M
Ford, *Rule of the Robots* (Basic Books, 2021)

72   M Chui, J Manyika, M Miremadi, 'Four fundamentals
of workplace automation', *McKinsey Quarterly*
(1 November 2015), www.mckinsey.com / capabilities /
mckinsey-digital / our-insights / four-fundamentals-of-
workplace-automation, accessed 14 June 2023

73   C O'Neil, *Weapons of Math Destruction: How big data increases
inequality and threatens democracy* (Crown Books, 2016)

74   'GreenPrint survey finds consumers want to buy eco-
friendly products, but don't know how to identify them',
Business Wire (22 March 2021), www.businesswire.com /
news / home / 20210322005061 / en / GreenPrint-Survey-
Finds-Consumers-Want-to-Buy-Eco-Friendly-Products-but-
Don%E2%80%99t-Know-How-to-Identify-Them, accessed
11 July 2023

75   IBM, *CEO Decision-making in the Age of AI* (CEO Study,
2023), www.ibm.com / thought-leadership / institute-
business-value / c-suite-study / ceo, accessed 7 June 2023

76   R Thaler and C Sunstein, *Nudge* (Penguin, 2009)

77   G Kawasaki, *The Art of the Start 2.0: The time-tested, battle-
hardened guide for anyone starting anything* (Penguin, 2015);
G Kawasaki, *Enchantment* (Penguin, 2012)

78   P Thiel and B Masters, *Zero to One* (Virgin Books, 2014)

Acknowledgements

I need to thank a number of individuals. Firstly and foremostly my wife, as without her patience, unconditional support and love, I do not think this book, or indeed my ongoing business pursuits, would be possible. Also my two daughters who make me proud every day and have provided valuable insights into Generation Z's digital needs and requirements.

To Maev Creaven who was a wonderful godmother to my eldest daughter, and was also my nutritionist, inspiring me to look at evidence first – an approach I apply to my health regime, business interests and this book. She was also a great pen pal over the last decade or so. I miss her daily.

A big thanks to all contributors to the case studies, which illustrate how innovative, agile and sustainable their businesses are thanks to their respective design, application and adoption of technology. Plus a huge thanks to Phil Young, Dr Greg B Davies, Alan Smith, Lee Robertson and Andrew Elson for their kind testimonials.

Finally, a big thank you goes to Bella, our faithful family hound, who has been by my side throughout the last sixteen years and kept me sane and in gratitude.

The Author

 Chris Davies MSc is an entrepreneur who founded Model Office, a regtech platform that serves over 1,000 firms in the financial market, and Engage Insight, a research business that employs evidence-based practice and data to industry projects. Prior to building his regtech business, Chris worked in the wealth management industry both in the UK and internationally. Chris published his first book, *Winning Client Trust,* in 2011 and writes and publishes articles in the industry press. His greatest achievement is his wonderful family.

🌐 www.culture-coding.com

in www.linkedin.com/in/chris-davies-msc-09b83711

✖ @ChrisatMOUK

🎙 https://podcasts.apple.com/gb/podcast/
id1527109526